9/24

FREAKIN' FABULOUS
on a BUDGET

How to dress, entertain, and decorate
in the style you so richly deserve

CLINTON
KELLY

GALLERY BOOKS

NEW YORK   LONDON   TORONTO   SYDNEY   NEW DELHI

ALSO BY CLINTON KELLY

FREAKIN' FABULOUS

OH NO SHE DIDN'T

G

Gallery Books
A Division of Simon & Schuster, Inc.
1230 Avenue of the Americas
New York, NY 10020

First Gallery Books hardcover edition October 2013

GALLERY BOOKS and colophon are registered trademarks of Simon & Schuster, Inc.

For information about special discounts for bulk purchases,
please contact Simon & Schuster Special Sales at 1-866-506-1949
or business@simonandschuster.com.

The Simon & Schuster Speakers Bureau can bring authors to your
live event. For more information or to book an event contact the
Simon & Schuster Speakers Bureau at 1-866-248-3049 or visit our
website at www.simonspeakers.com.

Design, illustrative typography, surface designs, and illustrations
by Jane Archer (www.psbella.com)

Photography © Steve Giralt

Manufactured in the United States of America

10 9 8 7 6 5 4 3 2 1

Library of Congress Cataloging-in-Publication Data

Kelly, Clinton.
Freakin' fabulous on a budget / Clinton Kelly.
pages cm
1. Etiquette. 2. Fashion. 3. Budgets, Personal. I. Title.
BJ1853.K455 2013
646.7—dc23
2013011680

ISBN 978-1-4767-1552-0
ISBN 978-1-4767-1553-7 (ebook)

CONTENTS

IN CLINTON WE TRUST

I have been broke,
and I have been rich.
But one thing has
never changed:
I HAVE ALWAYS BEEN

FABULOUS.

ecently I was interviewed for a newspaper article, and the reporter asked me what my life was like during graduate school. (I received my master's in journalism from Northwestern University.) I couldn't help but laugh when I recalled my first apartment in Chicago. It was the size of a walk-in closet, with two windows overlooking an alley. The kitchen had a two-burner stove and a half refrigerator. I slept on a backache-inducing futon and ate my meals while sitting on a folding chair at a card table. Those meals were usually something I cooked on Sunday and stretched to last most of the week.

And during it all, I thought I was the luckiest guy on earth. I was living in a spectacular city, making new friends, and learning one of the most important lessons of my life: Fabulousness has absolutely nothing to do with money.

Fabulousness comes from within. It's about living your life the most conscious way possible. Are the foods you're putting in your body the highest quality you can afford? Are the clothes you're wearing telling the world you're glad you got out of bed this morning? Does your abode make you happy the second you walk in the front door?

You want to be answering yes to those questions. I know you do. If you don't want to be eating well, dressing your body in a flattering way, and surrounding yourself with things that energize you, you've got a problem—and I'm not the guy to fix it. You probably need a therapist.

I honestly believe that each of us, at our core, wants to be a splendid version of ourselves. But modern society is constantly urging us to take the easy way out! Think about how simple it would be right now to grab a triple cheeseburger at the drive-through, go home and pull on a pair of sweatpants, and spend the rest of the day watching a *Hoarders* marathon from your couch.

And, look, I'm not judging. I have actually done a version of that. Who hasn't? But it rarely makes you feel good about yourself—because it's the opposite of fabulousness.

You know you'd be much happier if you ran to the supermarket in a cute pair of jeans, came home, whipped up a cassoulet, and made a terrarium for your windowsill! Omigod, I would so love you right now if you did that.

I've written this book with the hope that you'll be inspired to see the opportunities for fabulousness all around you. If I can do it, so can you!

XO Clinton

FOOD

PICTURE IT: SICILY, 1922.

My Salvatore and I are on our way to a feast. *Whoops. Sometimes I channel Sophia from The Golden Girls. I'll try again....*

PICTURE IT: LONG ISLAND, 1975.

My mother, Terri, dons her finest caftan and bell-bottoms to host a Tupperware party—avocado green and burnt orange are everywhere! And she puts out this spread of fabulous '70s hors d'oeuvres like Swedish meatballs and rumaki. The whole scene is pure heaven to six-year-old me, and I think,

I wish every day could be like this!

And that's the moment I know my future adult life will include hosting fabulous parties.

I love having people over to my place, and I know that I can't successfully entertain without serving great food. I also know that I can do it at a great price. This is the thing: A lot of fancy foods aren't really that fancy or expensive to prepare. In fact, many high-end foods have very lowbrow origins. You might pay ten bucks for a side of polenta at a fancy Italian restaurant, but it's still the same stuff poor farmers ate for centuries. And the next time you see a review for a sushi house charging hundreds of dollars, realize that those seaweed rolls began as cheap Japanese street food.

I also like to entertain because, quite frankly, I get off on impressing people with my mad entertaining skills. And you can too! People *really* don't expect much. I find that friends are actually kind of happy if you just order in a pizza and open a bottle of wine. While cost-effective, that's something people can do in their own homes. Instead, I like to offer people something homemade and delicious.

As it turns out, fabulousness is affordable when you have a few tricks under your apron. I'll show you mine if you show me yours.

YOU'RE INVITED :)

I have a policy of ignoring e-vites. Call me old-fashioned, but I want to be invited to a party by a human being with an actual pulse, not some computer program. Every invitation you send should be personalized—either by writing a guest's name on an envelope (remember those?) or via an email that you typed yourself. I want to read,

Dear Clinton,

I'm having a little get-together.

I hope you can come.

Then you can cut and paste the details. Is that too much to freakin' ask? Fifty-five characters, not including spaces. No, but you don't have time for that. You have to watch that *Real Housewives* marathon. Again.

CLINTON'S
THERAPY COUCH

"Whenever I host a dinner party, friends always ask me, 'What can I bring?' Even though I want to tell them to bring booze, as the host, I feel bad asking them to contribute. Is it all right to suggest that they bring a bottle of wine or is the only polite answer, 'Nothing. Just yourselves'?"

Well . . . it depends on what kind of party you're throwing, how many people you're having over, and how well you know your guests. A good host throws a dinner party so that his or her friends can have a relaxing, carefree evening. So, ideally, you should be prepared to have every aspect of that evening covered on your own. However, if you state in the invitation—even if it's a verbal one—that the party is potluck, then you can ask a guest to bring wine if she offers. You don't want to put your guests in the awkward situation of having to provide alcohol for everyone at your dinner table. Let's say you invite eight people over and only one friend asks if she can bring wine. You'd be better off buying the wine yourself, rather than charging her with the task or risking an awkward I-can't-afford-to-buy-that-much-wine moment. But if your group is close-knit and your dinner party is small and casual, feel free to accept a guest's generous offer. Just be sure to return the favor at her next party.

hors d'oeuvres

Give your appetizers
an instant upgrade by
calling them hors d'oeuvres.
Can't spell it? Who cares?
No one has asked you
to participate in a
spelling bee, just a small
dinner party, so relax.
GEEZ.

THE PERFECT CHEESE PLATE ▷—

Everybody likes cheese, unless you're lactose intolerant. And if you are, then my heart goes out to you. I wake up every morning and I thank the baby Jesus that I'm not lactose intolerant. Because I lo-o-ove cheese. A cheese plate is the easiest hors d'oeuvre you can make, or rather, put out. Add some bottles of wine and you have a simple gathering for friends. Done.

There's no right or wrong way to organize your dairy-licious selection—don't let the cheese snobs make you feel inferior. I serve the cheese I want to eat, quite frankly. But just like any great outfit hinges on color, pattern, texture, and shine, so does a cheese plate depend on some basic principles.

I make sure that they're different textures or, sometimes, made from different kinds of milk, whether sheep, cow, or goat, as well as different strengths. Try for a range of everything from mild to something with a little bit of a bite to it. Chat up the cheese guy at your supermarket. He wants to move the cheese before it goes bad (as in "serving a life sentence" bad), so there's always a cheese on special. Start with that well-priced hunk (the cheese, not the cheese guy) and build your selection from there. You don't need a pound of each cheese. People are fine with just one or two bites of each, which means you could serve a really small wedge of a really expensive cheese. Fabulous! If you're serving cheese as an appetizer or as a course, plan on about three ounces per person. And always serve cheese at room temperature, each with its own cheese knife.

Hot Tip

CHEESE PLATE POINTERS

For a stand-alone wine and cheese party, round out all that delicious dairy with an assortment of fresh breads and fruit, like sliced apples, pears, melon, grapes, or figs. If you're serving cheese before dinner, try savory accompaniments like olives and nuts. Get all Frenchy on your guests by serving cheese after dinner with dried apricots, dates, and fig chutneys or quince paste for a nice sweetness.

Hot Tip

MORE CHEESE PLATE POINTERS
Give your cheese plate a theme!
You can group by country (France,
Italy, United States, Botswana) or by
different kinds of milk (perhaps one each
of sheep, cow, and goat). Or group them
by type, like three different blues
or Bries. Here I've paired a mild
crumbly goat with a soft, medium-
strength triple crème
and a potent blue.

THE PERFECT ANTIPASTO PLATTER ▷•————————

People love meat! Except vegetarians, of course. There's something especially nice about the combination of booze and salty, cured meat. Sure, you could just throw together a platter of meats with Italian names and hope for the best, but you might end up with something unfabulous. As with cheese, you need to present a selection that varies in strengths from mild, like a mortadella, all the way up to a strong sopressata.

I know what you're thinking: "Clinton, you and your fancy meats—so pricey!" Sure, the cured variety can run up a bit more at the cash register, but you don't need to feed people half their weight in prosciutto! Fill in with wallet-friendly grilled seasonal vegetables, cheese, and bread.

Here are the basic building blocks for a *Freakin' Fabulous* antipasto platter:

Slices of cured meats such as capicola, salami, sopressata, mortadella, and prosciutto are a must

A variety of hard Italian cheeses like Parmigiano Reggiano, Grana Padano, and provolone, all cubed

Bocconcini (tiny mozzarella balls) can be mixed with a dressing of oil, fresh parsley, garlic, and red pepper flakes

Olives (see marinated olives on page 26)

Grilled vegetables and/or drained, jarred artichoke hearts and roasted red peppers

On a large platter, arrange items in a linear or pinwheel pattern, alternating meats, vegetables, and cheeses. Serve with sliced crusty Italian bread or focaccia. Mmm.

DUMPLINGS ▷

MAKES 24

The wheel. Q-tips. Wonton wrappers. They're all great inventions, but only one is your passport to serving *Freakin' Fabulous* appetizers. (It's the wonton wrappers, silly.) These little darlings will knock your guests' socks off with the help of two budget-friendly ingredients: frozen shrimp and ground pork (you need the flavorful fat in the dark meat that pricey all-white chops can't deliver). There's really not much that you can put in a dumpling that doesn't end up being delicious. Go crazy! These can be made ahead of time and frozen. Just reheat in some chicken stock when you are ready to serve them at your party.

1 pound medium shrimp, peeled and deveined

½ pound ground pork

1 tablespoon grated ginger

3 cloves garlic, finely chopped

¼ cup finely chopped scallions, plus more for garnish

1 egg

2 teaspoons cornstarch

1 tablespoon soy sauce

2 teaspoons sesame oil

24 wonton wrappers

½ cup chicken stock

Combine the shrimp, pork, ginger, garlic, scallions, egg, cornstarch, soy sauce, and sesame oil in a food processor and pulse until combined.

One at a time, wet the edges of a wonton wrapper with water. Add 1 tablespoon of filling to the center of the wrapper and begin pinching together the sides, leaving the center open-faced. Set on a baking sheet and cover with a damp towel until all the dumplings are assembled.

Over medium heat, coat a large skillet with vegetable oil. Add dumplings and cook for two minutes on one side and flip so the open center is facing down. Remove from skillet when crisp. Repeat until all dumplings are cooked. Carefully add chicken stock to skillet. Bring to a simmer. Return dumplings to skillet, cover and cook for 4 minutes. Serve with soy sauce, garnished with scallions.

HORS D'OEUVRES

FREAKIN' FABULOUS FONDUE ▷

SERVES 8

Fondue. I love a fondue! Oh. My. God. The best fondue I ever had was in Zermatt, Switzerland, on a mountain, overlooking the Matterhorn. But the first fondue I ever had was when I was about six, at that fateful Tupperware party. I remember thinking, "Bread dipped in cheese! What could be better than this?" Fondue is basically another way of setting out cheese and crackers, but instead of boring, fondue is *Freakin' Fabulous* and cheap, cheap, cheap.

1 tablespoon cornstarch

2 tablespoons Kirschwasser, or *kirsch*, German for "cherry water"

2 cups white wine

1 pound (about 4 cups) Gruyère or Swiss cheese, shredded

Dash of nutmeg

Bread cubes, sliced fruits and vegetables, roasted potato cubes for dipping

Add cornstarch to the Kirschwasser, or to a little white wine, and set aside. Heat wine in a medium saucepan over medium heat. Whisk in cornstarch mixture and simmer for 5 to 6 minutes. Fold in the cheese and nutmeg; stir until melted. If mixture is too thick, add more wine.

Transfer to a warm fondue pot.

Serve immediately with accoutrements like crusty bread, apples, kielbasa, fingerling potatoes, or steak tidbits.

For a big party, double or triple the recipe, set your slow cooker on low, and keep the extra fondue warm.

CHEAP TRICK

If you don't have Kirsch, leave it out. Or use the rest to make some Cherry Clafouti (page 88) too!

HORS D'OEUVRES

GOAT CHEESE AND ▷ RED PEPPER MOUSSE

MAKES 24 CRACKERS

I love the concept of taking cheap ingredients you have in the house and turning them into fancy hors d'oeuvres. You could bring the price tag of this mousse down further by eliminating the mascarpone, but it's so delicious, I suggest you eat any extra by the spoonful. Or in the summer, smear mascarpone on toast and top with a slice of garden-fresh tomato. OMG!

8 ounces goat cheese

4 ounces mascarpone or cream cheese

One 12-ounce jar roasted red peppers, drained and roughly chopped

1 teaspoon lemon zest

2 cloves roasted garlic

Salt and pepper to taste

Chopped chives, for garnish

Combine all ingredients in food processor, except chives, and mix until smooth, about one minute. Chill for 4 hours. Stir and add to pastry bag or plastic bag with the corner snipped off. Pipe onto crackers or bruschetta. Garnish with chopped chives and serve.

CLINTON'S THERAPY COUCH

Q *"Our home has a strict no-shoes policy. Is it rude to enforce this rule when I entertain?"*

A Oh, no one wants dog poop or chewing gum tracked into their home, but if you're completely neurotic about stuff like that, you probably shouldn't be hosting parties chez vous. A good hostess makes her guests feel as comfortable in her home as in their own. Some people don't want to walk around your house without footwear! I mean, how do I know your carpets are cleaner than my socks? And what if my big toe just punched a gaping hole through said sock? This is really stressing me out! Be a good girl and roll up the hand-knotted silk rug if you can't bear the thought of soles touching it. Or just do what I do when my guests leave: search the house with a black light, wearing a tool belt stocked with cleaning supplies.

HOT AND SPICY CHEESE TWISTS ▷———

MAKES 36 TWISTS

Like dark-wash denim, cheese twists are incredibly versatile. Not a fan of cheddar? I think you're a loon, but use Parmesan cheese instead. Just about any savory or sweet (think: cinnamon, sugar, and butter) combination will fancy up this frozen puff pastry. Serve them piping hot right out of the oven, and people will go ape shit. Twists can be made one day ahead, covered tightly in foil, and left at room temperature.

2 cups finely shredded cheddar cheese

1 teaspoon chopped, dried rosemary

¼ teaspoon dried, crushed red pepper flakes

Salt and pepper to taste

1 sheet (or half a 17.3-ounce package) frozen puff pastry, thawed

1 egg

1 tablespoon water

Preheat oven to 425°F. Place one rack in top third of the oven, the other in lower third. Line two large baking sheets with parchment paper.

Combine cheese, rosemary, red pepper flakes, and salt and pepper in a mixing bowl.

In a small bowl, whisk together the egg and water. Set aside.

Working on a floured surface, cut one piece of the pastry dough in half crosswise. Brush both rectangles with the egg wash. Distribute the cheese mixture evenly onto the pastry, pressing down lightly so it adheres to the dough.

Cut each half of dough lengthwise into ½-inch strips. Take two strips at a time and twist. Repeat with remaining strips.

Bake for 15 minutes or until golden and serve.

LEMON SHRIMP ▷

SERVES 12 AS AN APPETIZER

Who doesn't love shrimp? Well, besides people who are allergic to shellfish. And people who don't eat it for religious reasons. And vegans. Hmmm. Maybe I'm not selling this dish as strongly as I could, but I love it! I mean, I don't think I've ever thrown a shrimp-less shindig. Shrimp means you're fancy, and this recipe is easy and delicious. Save some dough by buying frozen farm-raised shrimp.

Zest of 1 lemon

½ cup lemon juice, from 2 large lemons

2 cloves garlic, crushed

1 tablespoon wine or sherry vinegar

2 tablespoons olive oil

12 green olives, pitted

1 small red onion, thinly sliced

Pinch of cayenne powder

1 to 1½ pounds large shrimp, peeled and deveined, thawed if frozen

2 to 3 teaspoons salt

In a large bowl, combine lemon zest, lemon juice, garlic, wine or vinegar, oil, olives, red onion, and cayenne powder.

Add salt to a pot of water and bring to a boil. Add thawed shrimp and boil for 1½ to 2 minutes, or until shrimp is pink and opaque. Remove immediately. Reserve a half cup of cooking liquid, then drain and place shrimp into marinade.

If needed, add a few tablespoons of the cooking liquid to the marinade. Cover and refrigerate for 2 to 3 hours, turning the shrimp once.

Serve on a platter with crusty bread or as individual portions in small bowls or parfait glasses. Bask in the light of your own fabulousness.

HORS D'OEUVRES

MARINATED OLIVES ▷

SERVES 8–10

Olives are a party staple but, like tan chinos, they can be really boring. Elevate these little ovals of flavor with some simple freshening up.

8 ounces mixed olives, drained

2 sprigs rosemary

Peel of 1 lemon, large strips (no pith, please)

½ cup olive oil

¼ cup red wine vinegar

1 clove of garlic, smashed

¼ teaspoon dried, crushed red pepper flakes

In an airtight plastic container, add olives, rosemary, and lemon peel. In a large measuring cup or bowl, add olive oil, vinegar, garlic, and red pepper flakes. Whisk together and pour over olives. Let marinate overnight or for several days.

Serve alone or as part of an antipasto platter.

WHAT ABOUT THE PITS?

Don't spit! Remove pits with aplomb. Bring the pit to the front of your mouth, put it between your teeth, and then extract it. You should probably use your left hand, because you might be shaking hands with your right. See, I think about these things. If you shake with your right and eat with your left, nobody's icky germs go into your mouth. And that, my friends, is why I never get sick.

Everyone hates that awkward moment of realizing you have an olive pit in your mouth and no idea where to put it. So, provide a pit receptacle near the olives. If you think your guests are particularly daft, craft a little sign, PUT YOUR PITS HERE. Or you could eat one olive yourself, and throw a pit into the dish to get things started. This way you won't be finding pits behind your throw pillows or in your houseplants.

HORS D'OEUVRES

MEXICAN CORN FRITTERS

MAKES 24 FRITTERS

I've been to Mexico twice. Both times I had a run-in with Montezuma. I don't know what I ever did to that guy, but evidently he hates me. I'm probably never going back to Mexico, but I refuse to deprive myself of fried corn. Such a bountiful combination for such a cheap, cheap price! These are totally fine whether deep-fried in a countertop fryer or just pan-fried in a little oil.

FOR THE CORN FRITTERS

One 7.5-ounce box corn muffin mix

½ cup all-purpose flour

1 tablespoon paprika

1 teaspoon cayenne pepper

½ cup milk

1 egg

½ stick unsalted butter, melted

1 small bunch scallions, grilled and chopped

1 cup corn kernels, grilled and fresh cut from the cob or frozen

Sea salt

FOR THE DIPPING SAUCE

¼ cup crumbled Cotija cheese (crumbled feta or shredded Parmesan cheese can be substituted)

½ cup mayonnaise

½ cup sour cream

1½ teaspoons Tabasco

Salt and pepper to taste

FOR THE CORN FRITTERS

Combine corn muffin mix, flour, paprika, and cayenne in a bowl. In a separate bowl, mix milk, egg, and melted butter, then add to dry ingredients. Stir in scallions and corn. In a Dutch oven, heat vegetable oil to 365°F. Drop batter by tablespoons into oil and fry until golden brown. Drain on paper towels. While still hot, sprinkle with sea salt and serve.

FOR THE DIPPING SAUCE

In a food processor, combine all ingredients and blend until smooth. Serve in a small bowl with the fritters.

SPICED CHICKPEAS ▷────────────────────

MAKES LOTS

Sometimes you feel like a nut. Sometimes you don't. These are for the times that you don't. These nibbly bits are almost on their way to becoming hummus . . . but stop short. The unfabulous among us would think, "Oh, I'll just throw out some hummus at my party." Boring! It's become ubiquitous and it's just not fancy anymore. These chickpeas: inexpensive, fancy, and probably the key to peace in the Middle East.

Two 19-ounce cans chickpeas, rinsed, drained, and patted dry with a paper towel

2 tablespoons olive oil

1 teaspoon cumin

1 teaspoon paprika (smoked if you've got it!)

½ teaspoon coriander

Dash of cayenne

Dash of cinnamon

Salt and pepper to taste

Toss chickpeas in olive oil. Combine all other ingredients in a bowl. Toss chickpeas with spices. Roast at 400°F for 30 to 35 minutes. Shake once to toss. Cool and serve.

THAI PORK LETTUCE CUPS ▷

MAKES 12 CUPS

I have never been propositioned for sex more often in my life than in Thailand. Even my waiter asked me to do the nasty. People in Thailand are highly sexed, so these lettuce wraps pretty much guarantee you'll get laid. I suggest using pork shoulder steaks because they are tasty and cheaper than pork loin by about $7 per pound.

1 pound pork shoulder steaks (about 4 steaks, ¼-inch thick)

5 tablespoons fish sauce

¼ cup fresh lime juice

3 teaspoons sugar

1 tablespoon ground, dried Thai chilies (or 1 fresh Thai chili or 1 scant teaspoon Sriracha sauce)

¼ cup crushed peanuts

1 small red onion, sliced into thin crescents

2–3 scallions, sliced thin

½ cup roughly chopped cilantro

⅓ cup roughly chopped mint leaves

½ seedless cucumber, julienned

1 large carrot, peeled and shredded

10–12 large leaves Boston lettuce or endive

Rub pork steaks with 2 tablespoons fish sauce and set in refrigerator for 30 minutes.

Meanwhile, to make dressing, whisk together 3 tablespoons fish sauce, lime juice, sugar, and chili or Sriracha. In a large bowl, combine peanuts, onion, scallions, cilantro, mint leaves, cucumber, and carrot. Add dressing and mix.

Grill or sauté pork steaks over high heat for 3 to 4 minutes on each side. Slice against the grain into long thin strips, cut into ½-inch pieces.

Add pork to dressing mix, toss, and serve in lettuce cups.

CHEAP TRICK

Herbs aren't cheap, I realize that. But they are incredibly inexpensive to grow, and quite easy. Plant yourself some thyme, rosemary, sage, mint, and basil this summer and you can enjoy fresh, FREE herbs all winter. Just freeze them in plastic bags. Dry them thoroughly and remove as much air as you can. You'll thank me in February. A card would be nice.

CHIPS, DIPS, CHAINS, WHIPS SERVES 8–10 ▷

These are my go-to dips. They're easy and inexpensive to make, and they *never* fail. And who doesn't love a good dip? Communists, that's who.

OUTRAGEOUS ONION DIP

2 tablespoons olive oil

2 large yellow onions, cut into ¼-inch-thick rings

Salt

1 clove garlic, finely chopped

1½ cups sour cream

¾ cup mayonnaise

Pepper

Heat the olive oil in a sauté pan over medium heat. Add the onions, season with a large pinch of salt, then toss to coat in oil.

Arrange the onions in an even layer in the pan, and cook, stirring occasionally, maintaining an even layer, until they caramelize, about 15 to 20 minutes. Remove from heat and stir in the garlic.

Combine the remaining ingredients in a food processor. Add the onions and garlic, and season with black pepper. Pulse until thoroughly combined. Chill in the refrigerator for several hours. Serve with potato chips and pretzels. But don't bother sharing with anyone. You will only resent them for eating the onion dip you could have eaten yourself.

WONDERFUL WHITE BEAN DIP

2 cans white cannellini beans, rinsed and drained

¼ cup olive oil

1 clove garlic

1 teaspoon dried rosemary

Zest of ½ a lemon

Salt and pepper to taste

Combine all ingredients in a food processor and pulse until smooth. Add more olive oil if needed.

Taste for salt. (It kind of needs a lot.) Serve with crostini or crudités. I love it with a Triscuit!

And Triscuit isn't even paying me to say that!

TANTALIZING TZATZIKI DIP

One 16-ounce container Greek yogurt

2 cucumbers, peeled, seeded, and grated

2 cloves garlic, minced

1 tablespoon olive oil

1 lemon, juiced

¼ cup chopped fresh dill or mint

Salt and pepper to taste

Drain yogurt in a bowl lined with paper towels. Cover and refrigerate for four hours or overnight. (If you skip this step, the dip still comes out delicious.)

Combine all ingredients, cover, and chill in the refrigerator for several hours. Serve with pita chips or crudités.

FREAKIN' FABULOUS *on a* BUDGET   34

SEASONAL
FOOD GUIDE

I have had enough of mealy pears! Don't try to serve me any more flavorless tomatoes. When fruits and veggies taste awful, they sit in your crisper and rot into a science experiment. It's money down the drain. But shopping for produce in season means the food costs less and tastes *Freakin' Fabulous*. Why? Food harvested in its prime growing season is abundant and happy. It's also less work for all of those hunky farmers to eke from the earth. All of that translates into reasonably priced, delicious food you'll be excited to cook. So grab your favorite recycled shopping bag and head over to your local farmers' market. Check out what's fresh and schmooze with the vendors for inside tips on what's at peak flavor. Think of it as a cost-efficient and fun way to expand your palate.

HERE'S A STARTER CHART OF WHEN FRUITS AND VEGGIES ARE IN SEASON

SPRING	SUMMER	FALL	WINTER
ARTICHOKES	BLUEBERRIES	SQUASH	SWEET POTATOES
ASPARAGUS	MELONS	BRUSSELS SPROUTS	GRAPEFRUITS
FAVA BEANS	PLUMS	MUSHROOMS	ORANGES
PEAS	APRICOTS	RUTABAGAS	CLEMENTINES
PINEAPPLE	CUCUMBERS	PEARS	PARSNIPS
RADISHES	TOMATOES	FIGS	PAPAYAS
RAMPS	PEACHES	APPLES	BROCCOLI RABE
RHUBARB	SUMMER SQUASH	CHARD	CAULIFLOWER
SPRING ONIONS	CHERRIES	KALE	BROCCOLI
WATERCRESS	BEETS	ONIONS	KOHLRABI
	BERRIES	CABBAGES	TURNIPS
		CARROTS	
		EGGPLANT	
		PUMPKIN	

sides

Some side dishes are so **GOOD** that people don't even want the main course. These are those sides.

STUFFED ARTICHOKES

MAKES 4

Most kids beg for chicken nuggets, mac 'n' cheese, or for their dad to stop eating so many beans. My sisters and I used to beg our mom to make artichokes. Whenever I think of eating an artichoke, I think about being outside on a gorgeous day with a glass of wine, leisurely putting each succulent leaf into my mouth. It's so glamorous to eat an artichoke! And it's a little bit sexy. You feel like you're breaking the rules when you're eating an artichoke. Even better, when you buy them in season, they are delightfully priced.

4 large artichokes

2 lemons

1½ cups bread crumbs

1 cup grated Parmesan cheese, plus ¼ cup for sprinkling

¼ cup chopped parsley

1 teaspoon each salt and pepper

5 cloves garlic, minced

5 tablespoons extra virgin olive oil

Preheat oven to 425°F.

Cut off the top ⅓ of each artichoke and cut off the stem to create a flat bottom. Remove all the tough leaves from the outside and snip off the prickly bits with kitchen scissors. Rub the artichoke with the juice from one of the lemons to prevent browning. Open the leaves of the artichoke with your thumbs, spreading the leaves apart so you can place the filling inside.

In a large bowl, combine bread crumbs, 1 cup of cheese, parsley, salt and pepper, garlic, and 1 tablespoon of olive oil. Mix until combined.

Place the artichokes in a medium baking dish. Sprinkle mixture over and inside the artichokes, moving the leaves around to get the mixture in between the leaves. Pour boiling water about 1 inch up the sides of the artichokes.

Spray a piece of aluminum foil with oil. Cover the baking dish tightly with the foil, oil side down. Bake for 45 minutes or until a knife pierces the bottom of the artichoke easily.

Remove from the oven and heat the oven to broil. Remove foil from the artichokes and sprinkle remaining cheese on top. Place under broiler for 2 to 3 minutes to brown.

Serve with lemon wedges.

LEMON-ROASTED ASPARAGUS ▷ WRAPPED IN PROSCIUTTO

SERVES 4–6

I'm gonna go out on a limb and say that asparagus is the fanciest vegetable that you can serve. Plus it's tall and thin and it will make you tall and thin. Not really. But we can pretend. In this preparation you're taking a very fancy-looking but not particularly expensive vegetable and wrapping it in a *very* fancy meat for a kick of flavor. The prosciutto is a big-ticket item, but when you use a small amount, it will cost you only a few dollars. Use a domestic variety, which is cheaper than imported.

1 bunch asparagus, washed, woody stems trimmed

Zest of 1 lemon

1 tablespoon olive oil

Salt and pepper to taste

6 thin slices prosciutto

Preheat oven to 400°F. Place asparagus on a baking sheet and toss with lemon zest, olive oil, and salt and pepper. Roast in oven for 10 to 12 minutes or until asparagus turns slightly golden. Shake pan once during cooking.

Bundle together 5 or 6 pieces of asparagus and wrap in a slice of prosciutto. Serve one bundle to each person.

CLINTON'S THERAPY COUCH

Q *"When I make water after eating asparagus it stinks up the whole room. Do I have to give up my favorite veggie for fear of someone catching a whiff of my pee-pee shame?"*

A Boy, do I love it when my fans overshare about their bodily functions. I will address this because I happen to know that pungent asparagus pee is genetic. While everybody's wee-wee has a strong smell after eating asparagus, only some people can actually detect the putrid odor. I, admittedly, can smell the nastiness. My dad, Mike, cannot, so feel free to eat a lot of asparagus in his house.

SIDES

Hot Tip

To prep asparagus,
bend the end of one stalk
and see where it snaps. Use this
as a guide for cutting or snapping
the rest of the bunch to remove
the tough, woody parts.
You can also peel the bottoms to
expose the tender parts.

BRUSSELS SPROUTS WITH BACON AND PARMESAN

SERVES 4

Brussels sprouts don't deserve their bad rap. Anyone who doesn't like them hasn't tried mine! I mean, they're sautéed in bacon fat, for crying out loud. Magnificent!

1 pound Brussels sprouts, rinsed, bottoms trimmed, and sliced in half

½ pound thick-cut bacon, cut into 1-inch cubes

1 shallot, finely chopped

1 tablespoon balsamic vinegar

¼ cup grated Parmesan cheese

Salt and pepper to taste

Blanch Brussels sprouts by cooking them for 1 to 2 minutes in salted boiling water, then plunging them into an ice-water bath and draining.

Meanwhile, place bacon in a skillet and cook over medium-high heat until crisp. Turn off heat and remove bacon to a plate lined with paper towels. Reserve 1 tablespoon of fat in the skillet and pour out the rest.

Add shallot and cook for 2 minutes over medium-high heat, then add Brussels sprouts and cook for 7 to 8 minutes until brown and tender. Add balsamic vinegar to deglaze pan and toss with Parmesan and salt and pepper.

Hot Tip

THE SALINE SOLUTION

Let's talk sodium. When you watch cooking shows, it always seems as though the chefs are adding a lot of salt. True, but it's probably kosher salt, which is not the same as the usual pinch of table salt. Kosher salt is less potent than the stuff your mother probably had on her spice rack. It's an easy upgrade, and one I'm glad I made, though I do miss that little girl with the umbrella on the Morton's packaging. She was my only friend for a short period in junior high.

SIDES

SAUTÉED CARROTS WITH FENNEL SEED

SERVES 4–6

I don't think you can find a less expensive vegetable than carrots. And most kids will eat them because they're kind of sweet. Who could object to a carrot, the most innocuous vegetable of all? I can't even imagine. That said, so many recipes call for just one carrot and then you have ten left over to wilt in a bag in the fridge. Annoying. And remember that bag of baby carrots you had the good intention of snacking on instead of Mallomars? I know you never even ate one. Use them with this preparation before they rot.

2 pounds carrots, peeled and trimmed

1½ tablespoons fennel seeds

2 tablespoons unsalted butter

½ cup chicken stock

¼ teaspoon nutmeg

Salt and pepper to taste

Cut the carrots on the diagonal into ¼-inch-thick pieces.

In a large, dry sauté pan, toast the fennel seeds over high heat for 1 to 2 minutes. Reduce heat to medium-high, add the butter, and when it is melted, add the carrots and the nutmeg.

Cook the carrots over medium heat until caramelized, about 5 to 7 minutes. Add the chicken stock and cover, allowing to steam for 5 minutes. Add salt and pepper. Serve immediately.

POTATO SALAD

SERVES 6–8

Many, many years ago, I worked in a Long Island deli, and in case you didn't know, that slop they pass off as potato salad comes out of a giant white bucket. It's repulsive. So why is this an awesome recipe for potato salad? Because I invented it! Mine is the best damn potato salad. Ever. Potatoes are also a great way to stretch your food budget.

And yes, if you're curious, I did operate a meat slicer at the deli and sliced off a small bit of my right thumb, which has since grown back nicely.

1 pound small red-skinned
new potatoes, quartered

Salt

2 tablespoons Dijon mustard

⅓ cup mayonnaise

¼ cup cooked crumbled bacon

¼ cup thinly sliced scallions

1 cup corn, fresh or frozen
and thawed

3 hard-boiled eggs, peeled
and chopped

Pepper

Place the potatoes in a large pot, cover with water, and add salt. Bring the water to a boil, then lower the heat to medium-low and simmer for 10 to 15 minutes, until the potatoes are just tender when pierced with a fork. Drain and let cool.

In a large serving bowl, combine all other ingredients, add the potatoes, mix thoroughly, and adjust seasonings. Can be served hot or cold.

SET THE TABLE!

Here is everything you need to know about setting the table: The fork goes to the left of the plate, the knife directly to the right of the plate with the blade facing the plate, the spoon to the right of the knife on the outermost right. (You'd be surprised how many people get that wrong.) Now, place your salad plate on top of your dinner plate, place your napkin on top of the salad plate, then add your salad fork to the left of your dinner fork. Next, place your soup spoon to the right of your teaspoon. Your wineglass sits above your spoons, your water glass to its left, and the bread plate sits above or to the left of the forks. Place your butter knife on top of your bread plate.

Voilà!

A perfectly set table. (That dude Barney who gives Julia Roberts the dinner etiquette lesson in *Pretty Woman* has nothing on me!)

SIDES

SCALLOPED SWEET POTATOES ▷

SERVES 6–8

Sweet potatoes are always on sale during the holidays and seem to last forever in the pantry. I recently found one from 1974. That's when it was all the rage to top sweet potatoes with marshmallows. Lose that recipe. Try this fresh one inspired by a meal I had in a café in Paris. Any opportunity to combine vegetables and cheese should not be missed.

1¾ cups heavy cream

1¼ cups shredded Gruyère or Swiss cheese

½ teaspoon nutmeg

Salt and pepper to taste

Butter for the baking dish

2 pounds sweet potatoes, peeled and cut into ⅛-inch rounds

¼ cup grated Parmesan cheese

Chopped scallions, for garnish

In a saucepan, heat the heavy cream over medium heat. Add 1 cup of shredded Gruyère or Swiss, the nutmeg, and salt and pepper. Cook, stirring, for 5 minutes.

Preheat oven to 400°F.

In a buttered casserole dish, place a layer of potatoes and then a layer of the cheese sauce. Repeat until all the potatoes and cheese sauce are used. Sprinkle the remaining ¼ cup shredded cheese and the grated Parmesan over the top.

Set the casserole dish on a cookie sheet and bake for 45 minutes, or until the sauce is bubbling and the top is golden brown. Cool for 10 to 15 minutes to allow potatoes to set, garnish with scallions, and serve.

SAVORY TOMATO CRUMBLE

SERVE 6–8

This dish is pure heaven in August and early September when tomatoes are at their peak of flavor. But it's delicious other times of the year too, because baking releases sugars from the fruit. If you find yourself with a plethora of green tomatoes at summer's end, feel free to use those! Just add a splash of your favorite vinegar and a sprinkle of sugar to cut down on the tartness.

3 pounds ripe but firm tomatoes

1 tablespoon all-purpose flour

2 garlic cloves, finely chopped

⅓ cup torn basil leaves, plus extra for garnish

2 tablespoons chopped fresh thyme

Salt and pepper to taste

1 cup bread crumbs

⅓ cup Parmesan or Romano cheese

¼ cup olive oil

Preheat oven to 400°F.

Cut the tomatoes into 8 round slices about ½-inch thick, remove seeds, and cut again into half-moons. In a large bowl, mix the tomatoes with the flour, garlic, basil, thyme, and salt and pepper. Pour tomato mixture into a casserole dish.

In a separate bowl, mix bread crumbs, cheese, and olive oil. Sprinkle topping over tomatoes.

Bake for 45 minutes or until golden brown. Cool for 10 minutes to allow tomatoes to set. Garnish with some freshly torn basil leaves.

CHEAP TRICK

To make your own bread crumbs, cube leftover bread, toast in the oven at 400°F until golden, and pulverize in a food processor. It will keep in the freezer for up to three months.

SIDES

TWICE-BAKED POTATOES ▷

SERVES 4

Mashed and baked. It's the best of both potato worlds! When I was a kid and my mom announced she was making these for dinner, I was instantly happy. Terri, this one is for you.

4 large russet potatoes, scrubbed

¼ cup cream cheese, softened

½ cup shredded cheddar cheese

2 tablespoons unsalted butter

Salt and pepper to taste

¼ cup chives, chopped, plus
1 tablespoon for garnish

2 pieces of bacon, crisply cooked
and roughly chopped

Preheat oven to 400°F. Using a fork, pierce the potatoes and place on a baking sheet. Bake for 45 minutes, then let cool for 10 minutes.

Cut potatoes in half lengthwise and, using an oven mitt or towel to protect your hand, scoop the potatoes out of their skins into a large bowl. Set the skins on the baking sheet, scooped-out side facing up.

Mash the potatoes, or even better, use a potato ricer. Add cream cheese, cheddar cheese, butter, salt and pepper, and ¼ cup chives. Spoon ¾ of the potato mixture back into the shells. Put the remaining potato mixture into a pastry bag with a star tip and pipe filling into each potato shell.

Return to oven and bake for 20 minutes. Sprinkle chives and bacon on top and serve hot.

CLINTON'S
THERAPY COUCH

Q *"I never have any fun at my parties! I worry that my food will taste like crap and no one will have a good time. How can I be the hostess with the mostest?!"*

A Let me let you in on the secret to my success: Don't stress out about anything that does not threaten your life or the life of a loved one. Why? Because life is too freakin' short. A party is a party, and you, my dear, will set its tone. When you're stressed, your guests will feel it. So do whatever it takes to chill the freak out. Take a Xanax. Have a pregame cocktail. Meditate. Have sex. Write another letter to Channing Tatum asking him to lift the restraining order. (Or all of the above, just as I do every Saturday night.) Serve the best food you can and do it with a smile. And tell everyone how good they look. You'll probably have to lie, but people love that shit.

DINNER
DOS & DON'TS

A FEW REMINDERS ABOUT EATING LIKE A CIVILIZED
HUMAN BEING, LIVING IN MODERN WESTERN SOCIETY

► **DO** Put your napkin on your lap as soon as you are seated.

► **DON'T** take the bread until you've offered it to other people at the table.

► If someone asks you to "pass the salt," pass both the salt and the pepper. They are a couple and don't like to be separated.

► Elbows off the table when there is food on the table. Before dinner, between courses, or after dinner, it's okay to lean on the table if you're engaged in a conversation. If you're just pouting like a twelve-year-old girl, not so much.

► Butter your bread by breaking off one mouthful at a time. **DON'T** slather the whole slice and keep the bread on the plate while buttering. No need to wave it in the air like you just don't care.

► Cut food, chew, swallow, repeat. **DON'T** start cutting your next piece until the last one has begun its trip through your digestive system.

► Always make sure to use a term of endearment when speaking to your waitress. For example, "I'll take the shrimp scampi, babe." Or "I'd like some more coffee, sugar tits."

(Kidding! Just wanted to see if you were paying attention. Don't do this.)

► When you're done with dinner, put your flatware like this

to signal that you've finished. **DON'T** stack your bread plate on your dinner plate, and for the love of all things holy, do not put your napkin on your plate! Also, **DON'T** help the server clear the table. That's his or her job. You can hand a server your plate if for some reason you're wedged way out of reach like the Xanax you dropped that rolled behind the toilet. Man, I hate it when that happens.

Are You Still Here?

You know what's really unfabulous? Talking to someone in person and occasionally checking your phone for text messages and social media. People who do that suck. I sat next to someone at a dinner party a few years ago. She thought she was a big deal because she was on *Dancing with the Stars* once. Now, I'm stuck next to this person because it's a freakin' dinner party and I'm doing my best to keep the conversation going—and let's face it, I'm a master at small talk. I can do it like it's my freakin' job. Well, this chick has the nerve to pick up her phone and check her text messages while I'm in the middle of a story.

I turned my back to her and didn't talk to her for the rest of the dinner. The next time someone does this to you, shun her. Treat her like Demi Moore in *The Scarlet Letter* . . . speaking of which, who the hell cast her in that movie?

Oh, no you didn't, beotch!

entrées

Order any of these main
courses when dining out and
you'll probably overpay. Cook
them at home to stretch your
money and give your taste
buds an orgasm. For a small
extra charge, I can come to
your house and serve them to
you while wearing my sexy
French waiter costume.

BEEF BOURGUIGNON

SERVES 6–8

Do not let foreign-sounding names fool you. Here in America we just call this dish beef stew, but your friends will be more impressed when you call it *beouf*! (Rhymes with "hoof.") This streamlined version of the meal made famous by Julia Child has a lot of ingredients, but using frozen veggies will cut down on the cost. No matter how you make it, to my mind this is the perfect dish for a small dinner party. This is really one of those meals that just says "Love." I think it's the fanciest comfort food that I've ever had. Serve with mashed potatoes or buttered, parsleyed potatoes.

1 bay leaf

3 sprigs fresh thyme

3 sprigs parsley

1 tablespoon olive oil

½ small yellow onion, or 1 shallot, chopped

¼ pound thick-cut bacon, diced

1½ pounds stewing beef, cut into 1½-inch cubes

¼ cup all-purpose flour

1½ cups beef stock

1¼ cups red wine

½ cup sliced mushrooms

1 cup chopped carrots

1 cup pearl onions

1 cup peas

Salt and pepper to taste

Tie together the bay leaf, thyme, and parsley to make a *bouquet garni*. Set aside. If you opt to use dried herbs, use a teaspoon each of parsley and thyme.

In a Dutch oven, heat the olive oil over medium heat. Add onion (or shallot) and bacon and cook until slightly browned. Remove from the pan and set aside, reserving the fat in the Dutch oven.

Toss the beef in the flour and cook in pan until browned. Don't overcrowd the pan. You may need to brown the beef in two or three batches.

Meanwhile, in a small saucepan, heat the stock until just under a boil.

Deglaze the Dutch oven with red wine, scraping the bottom of the pan as you pour. Add hot stock, *bouquet garni*, mushrooms, carrots, reserved bacon and sautéed onion, pearl onions, and peas. Cover and simmer gently for 2 to 2½ hours.

ENTRÉES

CHEAP TRICK

When you see packaged stew meat at the supermarket, chances are you're paying extra for the convenience. Save some dough by asking the butcher for chuck roast and cut it into cubes yourself. Whatever you don't use, throw in the freezer for next time.

BRACIOLE

SERVES 6–8

This dish speaks to my Italian roots. Right now I am pronouncing its name (bra-ZHOLE) while using many hand gestures. And, like my Italian ancestors, I serve my lightly dressed salad *after* the main course and on the same plate so all of the yummy braciole juices don't go to waste.

1 flank steak, about 1½ to 2 pounds

Salt and pepper to taste

½ cup Romano cheese

½ cup Parmesan cheese

½ cup bread crumbs

1 tablespoon fresh thyme leaves

1 garlic clove, finely chopped

5 tablespoons olive oil

1 cup beef stock (white or red wine works too)

3 cups Quick, Fresh Tomato Sauce

Salt and pepper to taste

Chopped parsley, for garnish

Preheat oven to 325°F.

Place flank steak on a cutting board and season both sides with salt and pepper. In a bowl, combine the cheeses, bread crumbs, thyme, garlic, and 3 tablespoons olive oil. Sprinkle the stuffing evenly over the top of the flank steak, and press down to keep the stuffing together. Starting at one small end, roll the steak up and secure with butcher's twine.

In a large, deep, ovenproof sauté pan, heat 2 tablespoons oil over medium-high heat and brown the braciole on all sides. Add the stock and bring to a boil. Add the tomato sauce and cover the dish with foil.

Place the sauté pan in the oven and cook for 1½ hours, turning and basting the meat every 30 minutes. Remove the foil and cook for 30 more minutes.

Remove the braciole from the pan, wrap in foil, and allow to rest for 10 minutes. Snip twine and cut the meat roll into 1-inch-thick rounds. Garnish with chopped parsley.

QUICK, FRESH TOMATO SAUCE

10 on-the-vine tomatoes

1 onion, diced

2 garlic cloves, finely chopped

½ cup torn basil leaves

Salt and pepper to taste

Blanch tomatoes by submerging in boiling water for 2 minutes, then drain and shock in an ice-water bath. Peel and seed tomatoes, then chop and set aside. In a large sauté pan, add the onion and garlic, and cook for 2 to 3 minutes or until fragrant. Add the chopped tomatoes. Season. Simmer for 10 to 15 minutes. Stir in the basil and serve.

BUTTERNUT SQUASH RAVIOLI WITH BROWNED BUTTER AND SAGE

SERVES 4–6

I'm telling you right now, after you make this dish, you're going to say, "I can't believe I just made that! It's delicious! I'm a star!" It's the same pasta you'd pay $24 for in a nice restaurant, but you can serve your whole family for a small fraction of that. This is why so many chefs drive nicer cars than you. Kidding! Sort of. Did I mention it's brown butter and sage? The most delicious duo since Sonny and Cher.

2 pounds butternut squash, diced

½ cup pecorino Romano cheese, plus more for garnish

1 teaspoon cinnamon

1 teaspoon nutmeg

1 egg

Salt and pepper to taste

2 packages wonton wrappers

1 stick unsalted butter

10 sage leaves

In a saucepan, boil enough salted water to cover the squash. Cook the squash for about 10 minutes or until completely tender. Remove the squash and set aside. Save the water to boil your ravioli later.

In a large bowl, mix the cheese, cinnamon, nutmeg, and egg together, and add salt and pepper to taste. Add the butternut squash and mix until thoroughly combined.

Working with two wrappers, wet each edge with water, place 1 tablespoon filling into the center of one wrapper and, matching wet edges together, place the second wrapper on top, forming a large square ravioli. Repeat with remaining wonton wrappers until all the filling is used.

In a large sauté pan, melt butter and add sage leaves. Cook over low heat for 10 to 15 minutes. When the butter begins to have little brown bits throughout, it is ready.

Cook the ravioli in gently boiling water for 2 to 3 minutes. Drain and toss in the brown sage butter and serve.

ENTRÉES

CASSOULET

Cassoulet (cass-ooh-LAY) sounds fancy, right? It's not. This is just more peasant food, people. It might sound like you could get this only in a snooty French restaurant, but the name simply refers to the dish it is cooked in. This simplified version is one that came to me on a gray autumn day when I had a real craving for cassoulet. I needed a delicious food to smell delicious in the house all day and lift my spirits more than half a Xanax. It was as though French angels spoke through me that day, magically transforming me into a 1950s French housewife named Babette.

6 boneless chicken thighs

Salt and pepper to taste

3 tablespoons olive oil

1 medium onion, chopped

6 garlic cloves, peeled and smashed

3 carrots, peeled and chopped into large dice

1 tablespoon dried rosemary

1 tablespoon dried thyme

1 tablespoon crushed red pepper flakes

2 chorizo sausages, cooked and cut into cubes

2 cans navy beans in water, drained

One 28-ounce can crushed San Marzano tomatoes

½ cup bread crumbs

¼ cup Parmesan cheese

Season the chicken with salt and pepper, then in a Dutch oven, over high heat, add the olive oil and brown, 2 minutes per side. Remove from the pot and set aside on a plate.

Reduce heat to medium-high and add the onion, garlic, carrots, rosemary, thyme, red pepper flakes, and chorizo. Sauté 3 to 4 minutes. Add navy beans and crushed tomatoes and cook to heat through. Return the chicken and drippings back to the pot and cook for 2 hours at 300°F.

Remove from the oven, stir—the chicken should fall apart—and ladle into ramekins. Top with bread crumbs and Parmesan and brown under the broiler. If you don't have ramekins, just top the stew with bread crumbs and cheese in the Dutch oven and broil, then spoon individual servings into nice bowls.

Serve with crusty bread.

CHEAP TRICK

This recipe calls for boneless chicken thighs, but the bone-in chicken thighs are less expensive. So, just buy them with the bones and take those suckers out yourself to make chicken stock.

ENTRÉES

CHICKEN CORDON BLEU ▷
EN CROUTE SERVES 4–8

The first time I ever had chicken cordon bleu was on an airplane flying from New York to San Francisco to visit my grandparents—I was eleven. Keep in mind this was airline food, but it was so exciting to be served this grown-up-sounding meal and to be flying by myself. In reality, it was probably disgusting, but in my mind, it was amazing. Here I offer you my much tastier version, swaddled in puff pastry for some extra flair.

FOR THE CHICKEN

1 package frozen puff pastry

4 boneless, skinless chicken breasts

Salt and pepper to taste

1 tablespoon unsalted butter

1 tablespoon olive oil

4 thin slices of ham

8 pieces Swiss cheese

1 egg, lightly beaten

FOR THE SAUCE

2 tablespoons unsalted butter

1 small shallot, finely chopped

2 tablespoons all-purpose flour

½ cup white wine

1 cup chicken broth

FOR THE CHICKEN

Preheat oven to 400°F.

Cut the pastry into four even pieces. On a lightly floured surface, roll out each piece of the puff pastry to roughly double its size.

Season the chicken with salt and pepper. In a sauté pan, heat the butter and oil on high heat and brown the chicken on both sides. Set the chicken aside to cool slightly.

To each piece of puff pastry, add a piece of ham, then two pieces of cheese, and finally the chicken. Fold in all the corners to seal, trim away excess dough, and flip onto a baking sheet lined with parchment paper. Brush with egg wash and bake for 30 minutes until crust is golden.

FOR THE SAUCE

To the drippings, over medium-high heat, add the butter and cook the shallot until browned. Stir in the flour to form a roux. Deglaze the pan with the wine and cook for 1 to 2 minutes, stirring constantly. Add the chicken broth and cook, stirring, over medium heat until the sauce is reduced by half.

Spoon over the chicken and serve. These beauties are large enough to cut in half and serve one half to each guest.

CURRIED CHICKEN SALAD IN A CREAM PUFF SHELL

SERVES 8

Cream puff shells are my obsession. I like them with ice cream, I like them with pastry cream, I like them with whipped cream, and I like them with chicken salad. They are instant food elevators and make everything fancy. This curried chicken salad is great for a light luncheon because the flavor combination is a little bit exotic with the sweet and savory bound together by thick Greek yogurt. I imagine myself eating this with Dinah Shore, and both of us breaking into the song "Ladies Who Lunch." She actually did that with Jane Russell. I'm so jealous!

FOR THE CHICKEN SALAD

½ cup mayonnaise

⅓ cup Greek yogurt

5 teaspoons curry powder

1 tablespoon fresh lime juice

1 teaspoon honey

1 teaspoon ginger, minced

Salt and pepper to taste

4 boneless, skinless chicken breasts, poached and cubed or shredded

1 small red onion, diced

1 green apple, diced

½ cup golden raisins

½ cup salted, roasted cashews, coarsely chopped

Chives, for garnish

FOR THE CREAM PUFFS

1 cup water

1 stick unsalted butter

1 cup all-purpose flour

4 eggs

FOR THE CHICKEN SALAD

In a large bowl, whisk together the mayonnaise, yogurt, curry powder, lime juice, honey, ginger, and salt and pepper. Add the chicken, onion, apple, raisins, and cashews and stir gently to combine.

FOR THE CREAM PUFFS

Preheat oven to 400°F.

In a medium saucepan, heat the water and butter until just boiling. Turn down to a simmer and, stirring constantly, add the flour gradually, ¼ cup at a time. The mixture will become a big ball. Let cool to room temperature.

Transfer the dough to a mixing bowl and, using an electric beater on low, add the eggs one at a time, waiting until each egg is incorporated before adding the next. Beat until smooth and velvety.

Lightly coat a cookie sheet with nonstick spray or use a silicone liner.

Drop the batter in 8 large spoonfuls on the cookie sheet and cook for 45 minutes until medium-golden brown and dry on the outside. Or make 12 smaller puffs and cook for 35 minutes.

Split the cream puffs in half and fill with chicken salad. Garnish with chives and serve.

CHEAP TRICK

Got a leftover chicken roaster? Knock yourself out. Curried chicken salad is a great way to use it and liven it up. The next time you roast a chicken, make two! You've got the oven going anyway, so why the hell not?

COQ AU VIN

SERVES 4—6

This is simply chicken in sauce but it sounds better when you say COKE-oh-VAN. A good gravy will make the meat moist and flavorful so no one at the table will complain, "Not chicken again, Ma!" Let's face it, chicken is very budget-friendly and this is a nice way to change up a food that you might be serving on a regular basis. It's also fab for company, because you can keep it on the stove longer than the prescribed 30 minutes. Make it before everybody gets there and keep it on low on the back of the stove. When it's served, your guests will exclaim, "How did she have the time to do this?" Meanwhile, you've been sitting around polishing your nails and delinting your couch while the bird was resting.

4 thick-cut bacon slices, chopped into ½-inch cubes

4 tablespoons all-purpose flour, divided

Salt and pepper to taste

1 roaster chicken cut into 8 parts and skin removed

One 10-ounce package cremini mushrooms, wiped clean and chopped into quarters

1 large or 2 small carrots, peeled and roughly chopped into rounds

6 cipollini onions, peeled and cut in half, or 1 medium yellow onion, sliced

1 clove garlic, finely chopped

2 cups light-bodied red wine

One 14.5 ounce can chicken broth

1 bay leaf

In a Dutch oven, sauté the bacon cubes over medium-high heat until crisp. Remove bacon with a slotted spoon and set on a paper towel–lined plate, reserving the bacon fat. Turn the heat up to high. Mix together 2 tablespoons flour and salt and pepper to taste and pat over the chicken parts. Brown the chicken in the bacon drippings, about 5 to 7 minutes. Once browned, remove to a plate.

If the pot is too dry, deglaze with a couple tablespoons of chicken broth. Add the mushrooms, carrots, and onions and sauté until brown, then add the garlic. Sprinkle the vegetables with the remaining 2 tablespoons flour and cook on medium-high heat for 1 to 2 minutes. Add the wine, chicken broth, bay leaf, and salt and pepper to taste and bring to a simmer. Scrape the pot to release the brown bits. Simmer for 5 minutes.

Return the chicken pieces to the pot, reduce heat to medium, and cook, without a cover, for 20 to 25 minutes. Serve over mashed potatoes or egg noodles.

CHEAP TRICK

PUT IT ON ICE

If you buy a box of soup stock or if you make your own, you're probably not going to use it all for one dish. Don't pour it down the drain along with your money. Freeze it! Fill an ice cube tray and in an hour or so, pop the ice cubes out individually, put them in a plastic bag, and you can use the stock as needed. Or you can treat the kids to frozen stock-pops. "Mmmm, Mom, yummy chicken flavor!" Just kidding. Kids would hate that.

HALIBUT À LA GRENOBLOISE

SERVES 4

Don't whine about not liking fish. Just try this preparation, then come crawling back to me. You can use any firm, white fish in this recipe (tilapia, turbot, flounder) because the fancy flavor profile of the butter, capers, and citrus sauce is sensational. (FYI, it's pronounced gren-oh-BLWAHZ.)

2 grapefruits, peeled

2 cups all-purpose flour

Salt and pepper to taste

2 eggs, lightly beaten

2 cups bread crumbs

4 halibut fillets

4 tablespoons olive oil

½ stick unsalted butter

4 teaspoons capers, drained

1 tablespoon minced shallot

¼ cup chopped fresh flat-leaf parsley

1 tablespoon highest-quality extra-virgin olive oil

Juice one of the grapefruits and set the juice aside in a bowl. Using a knife, peel the white pith off the other grapefruit, then, over the bowl to catch the juices, cut between the membranes to release the segments, and set aside the segments. Squeeze the remaining membranes to release the juice into the bowl.

Arrange three shallow dishes: in one dish, mix the flour with salt and pepper; in the second dish, your lightly beaten eggs; in the third, the bread crumbs.

Dredge the fish lightly on each side in the flour, then the eggs, then the bread crumbs.

Heat 4 tablespoons olive oil over medium-high heat. Add the fish, cooking for 2 to 3 minutes per side, until golden brown. Remove to a paper towel–lined plate. Drain the pan and wipe clean.

Add the butter, and once foam has subsided, add the capers, shallot, and grapefruit juice and heat through. Stir and remove from the heat.

In a bowl, combine the parsley, extra-virgin olive oil, and the grapefruit segments. Toss with salt and pepper to taste.

Spoon the sauce over the fish, and top with the grapefruit-parsley salad to serve.

ENTRÉES

SALMON EN PAPILLOTE SERVES 4 ▷

Cooking *en papillote* (ahn pap-ee-OAT) is simply wrapping food in parchment paper and allowing it to self-steam in the oven. Everyone loves getting presents, and this dish comes neatly wrapped like a gift. The process of eating it is an experience in itself. As long as you've got onions and lemon zest, you can add or remove any ingredient as you desire. If you want to throw in some asparagus tops, go for it, because it's basically going to steam and take on the flavor of the sauce.

1 fennel bulb, thinly sliced

1 lemon, zested and juiced

1 medium onion, cut in half and sliced into thin half-moons

2 garlic cloves, finely chopped

½ cup kalamata olives, pitted and roughly chopped

1 can diced San Marzano tomatoes, drained

1 tablespoon herbes de Provence

2 tablespoons extra-virgin olive oil

4 salmon fillets, about 6 ounces each

Salt and pepper to taste

Parchment paper

Preheat oven to 350°F.

Combine all the ingredients except the salmon and salt and pepper in a large bowl and toss gently to combine.

Cut parchment paper into four 15-inch squares. Place a salmon fillet on each parchment square and season with salt and pepper. Top each piece of fish with ¼ of the fennel mixture.

Wrap the parchment paper around the fish and tie tightly with butcher's twine. Place the packets on a baking sheet and cook for 30 minutes.

Place a packet on each diner's plate and serve with roasted new potatoes, garnished with dill. You could also cook the potatoes in each packet, just be sure to slice them very, very thin.

CHEAP TRICK

Herbes de Provence is fairly expensive to buy (those French are fabulous but also know how to inflate prices), but you can make it yourself: it's simply a mixture of dried thyme, rosemary, savory, marjoram, and lavender. You probably have thyme, rosemary, and possibly marjoram in your kitchen already. Use it. But please, don't puncture that sachet in your hall closet to harvest the lavender. Use organic culinary lavender.

STEAK FRITES WITH BÉARNAISE SAUCE ▷ SERVES 4

Hanger steaks are the cut butchers used to keep for themselves. Why? Because they were inexpensive and full of flavor. Then everybody learned their secret and started talking about those damn, greedy butchers. I like to imagine the French Revolution starting over this dish.

FOR THE STEAK
2 tablespoons unsalted butter

One 2-pound hanger steak

Salt and pepper to taste

Chopped chives, for garnish

FOR THE FRIES
3 large russet potatoes, skin on and scrubbed

Vegetable oil, for frying

Salt

FOR THE BÉARNAISE SAUCE
¼ cup chopped fresh tarragon leaves

2 shallots, finely chopped

¼ cup dry white wine

¼ cup champagne vinegar

4 egg yolks

Salt and pepper to taste

1 stick unsalted butter, melted

FOR THE STEAK
In a large skillet, melt the butter over high heat. Season the steak with salt and pepper. Add the steak to the skillet and brown on both sides. For a medium-rare steak, cook for 6 minutes on each side, cook for 1 more minute per side for medium, and 2 to 3 more minutes per side for well-done. Tent steak with foil and let it rest for 5 to 10 minutes.

Slice the steak against the grain and serve on a platter with fries alongside. Drizzle béarnaise sauce over the top or present the sauce in a serving vessel. Garnish with chives and serve immediately.

FOR THE FRIES
Heat the oil in a Dutch oven to 365°F. Using the julienne attachment on a mandoline, cut the potatoes into thin strips and fry until golden brown.

Drain on a paper towel–lined plate and immediately sprinkle with salt. Serve alongside the steak.

FOR THE BÉARNAISE SAUCE
In a saucepan, over medium heat, cook the tarragon, shallots, wine, and vinegar together until the liquid is reduced by half. Remove from heat and allow to cool.

In a blender, on the lowest speed, blend the egg yolks, tarragon reduction, and salt and pepper for 20 seconds. Remove the center of the blender lid and slowly pour in the melted butter and blend until combined.

CHICKEN VOL-AU-VENT SERVES 4 ▷

Vol-au-vent (VOLE-oh-VAHN) means "flight in the wind." How do I know? Because I'm fluent in French . . . and it's in the dictionary. I first learned about vol-au-vent as a sixteen-year-old busboy on Long Island. Every time I heard someone tell their waiter, "I'll have the vol-au-vent," I would think, "One day I'm going to be rich enough to have the vol-au-vent." Well, as it turns out, I've made a nice living in television, so I've had my fair share of vol-au-vent. It's good! And pretty easy to make. Cheap, too—that was the biggest surprise. Impress your friends with this recipe. You can borrow my busboy story if you want.

1 cup chicken stock

1 bay leaf

2 boneless, skinless chicken breasts

Salt and pepper to taste

½ stick unsalted butter, divided

1 large shallot, finely chopped

½ pound mushrooms, wiped clean, trimmed, and sliced

1 clove garlic, finely chopped

1 tablespoon all-purpose flour

2 tablespoons sherry (or any dry red wine)

2 tablespoons Dijon mustard

¼ cup heavy cream

1 teaspoon paprika

½ cup fresh parsley, chopped

6 vol-au-vent shells

In a saucepan, bring the chicken stock and bay leaf to a boil. Set aside. Meanwhile, cut the chicken into ½-inch cubes and season with salt and pepper. Heat 2 tablespoons of butter over medium-high heat and sauté the chicken pieces until golden and cooked through, about 4 to 5 minutes. Remove from the pan and set aside.

To the hot pan, add the remaining butter and sauté the shallot for about 2 minutes, then add the mushrooms and cook until they're golden brown, about 5 minutes. Add the garlic and cook for another minute. Sprinkle the flour over the vegetables and stir, add the sherry, and cook until the flour is absorbed.

Add the stock and chicken, stirring as the sauce thickens. Add the mustard, heavy cream, paprika, and salt and pepper, and stir for another minute more. Stir in the parsley and pour the mixture into the vol-au-vent shells. Serve piping hot.

Hot Tip

If you have trouble finding vol-au-vent shells, use frozen puff pastry dough and a large, round, 6-inch cookie cutter to cut shells, bake, and fill with your chicken mixture.

ENTRÉES

desserts

Life's too short to skip dessert.
Life's also too short to
surround yourself with idiots.
Or to wear bad shoes.
These are some of my favorite
SWEET treats that will add
a little more fabulousness
to your palate.

APPLE CROSTATA

SERVES 6–8

Can't find your favorite pie dish but still crave homemade apple pie?
Me too. Well, apple crostada it is!

1 refrigerated 9-inch piecrust (the rollout kind)

3 to 4 Granny Smith apples (to make 4 cups), peeled and cut in ¼-inch slices

1 tablespoon each lemon zest and juice

2 tablespoons all-purpose flour

2 teaspoons cinnamon

1 teaspoon vanilla extract

½ cup sugar, plus 1 tablespoon for dusting

¼ teaspoon salt

Dash of nutmeg

1 egg, beaten

Preheat oven to 450°F.

Place the piecrust on a cookie sheet lined with parchment paper or sprayed with cooking spray.

In a large bowl, combine the apples, lemon zest and juice, flour, cinnamon, vanilla, sugar, salt, and nutmeg. Pour filling into the center of the piecrust, leaving a 2-inch border. Fold the 2-inch border up over the apples to form a crust.

Brush the crust with the egg and sprinkle on sugar.

Bake for 25 minutes, or until crust is golden brown and apples are tender.

Serve with vanilla ice cream and a shower of toasted nuts, garnished with mint.

STOP FLAPPING YOUR GUMS

One of the keys to fabulousness is maintaining an air of mystery. You don't need to tell your guests about every little money-saving trick. For example, when it comes to baking a pie, I'll occasionally get a store-bought crust. (Shhh. Let's keep that between us.) I just customize it to make it look more homemade. Here's how to do it.

1. Buy a frozen crust made with butter.
2. Let it thaw.
3. Cut off the machine-made edge with a paring knife.
4. Carefully remove the remaining crust from the pie tin, and lay it in your own cute pie dish.
5. Patch any cracks with water.
6. Crimp the edges with your fingers so it looks homemade.
7. Bake.
8. When your guests tell you the crust is great, say, "Thank you!"

DESSERTS

BOOZY SHAKES

MAKES 2 SHAKES

Remember when you were a kid and a milk shake could brighten your whole day? And remember being an adult who just really needed a stiff drink? Well, whaddya know . . . now you can have the best of all possible worlds—ice cream and alcohol living together happily ever after.

BASIC BOOZY SHAKE BASE

⅓ cup milk

2 cups vanilla ice cream

Combine in a blender with the mix-ins of your choice. Blend on medium speed, stopping to stir several times with a long spoon, if necessary, to help the ingredients blend well.

Add more or less milk or ice cream to reach your desired consistency.

Top with whipped cream and add a garnish.

MIX-INS

FAST FOOD SHAKE

4 tablespoons chocolate drink mix

1.5 ounces chocolate liqueur

1.5 ounces dark rum

GRASSHOPPA!

3 tablespoons chocolate syrup

1.5 ounces chocolate liqueur

1.5 ounces crème de menthe

BOURBON PEACH

2 ounces bourbon

1 ounce peach Schnapps

Dash of cinnamon

BOURBON CARAMEL

3 tablespoons caramel sauce

3 ounces bourbon

COFFEE BREAK

Reduce milk to ¼ cup

¼ cup cooled strong coffee or espresso

3 ounces coffee liqueur

LEMON TWIST

Reduce milk to ¼ cup

Zest of 1 lemon

¼ cup limoncello liqueur

BRIOCHE BREAD PUDDING

SERVES 8–10

This gooey bread pudding is my kind of dessert. Remnants of Italian bread, extra challah after the holiday, or day-old croissants are all viable options here. No bread left behind! For the *most* economic version of this recipe, stash extra dinner rolls in your purse when you're out at a restaurant and use them the next day.

FOR THE BREAD PUDDING

½ loaf brioche bread, cubed (about 4 cups)

Butter for the baking dish

3½ cups whole or low-fat milk

4 eggs (or substitute egg whites for 1 or 2 of the eggs)

2 tablespoons bourbon

1 teaspoon vanilla extract

1 teaspoon cinnamon

¼ teaspoon salt

Dash of nutmeg

FOR THE BOURBON BANANA SAUCE

1 stick unsalted butter

1 cup brown sugar

½ teaspoon cinnamon

1 teaspoon vanilla extract

4 bananas, peeled and cut into 1-inch-thick slices

¼ cup bourbon

FOR THE BREAD PUDDING

Place the bread cubes in a 9-by-12-inch buttered baking dish. In a large bowl, whisk together the rest of the ingredients for 3 to 4 minutes, until well combined and slightly foamy.

Pour the custard over the cubes and press cubes down with a spatula or spoon. Let stand for 30 minutes. Stir the bread pudding to mix the cubes and custard, press down again, and let stand for 30 more minutes.

Meanwhile, preheat the oven to 350°F. Place the pudding baking dish in a roasting pan with an inch of hot water covering the bottom, and bake in oven until golden brown on top, about 40 minutes. Set aside to cool.

FOR THE BOURBON BANANA SAUCE

In a saucepan over medium-high heat, add the butter, brown sugar, cinnamon, and vanilla, and simmer until the sugar is dissolved. Add the sliced bananas and allow to caramelize.

Turn the heat down to medium-low and add the bourbon. Cook for 2 to 3 more minutes.

Meanwhile, cut the cooled bread pudding into squares and pour sauce on top to serve. This is also delicious reheated for breakfast with maple syrup on top.

CHERRY CLAFOUTI ▷─────────────────

SERVES 8

This is my take on a Julia Child classic. Just mention her name to guests as your inspiration and you could serve crap on rye and everyone would still rave. Clafouti (cla-FOO-tee) originated in central France in the nineteenth century. Wasn't fancy then, but it is now (even though it's really just a big cherry pancake)! I like to elevate its status by slicing it into pretty triangles before serving.

1¼ cups milk

½ cup sugar

3 eggs

1 tablespoon vanilla extract

1 tablespoon Kirsch (cherry liqueur)

⅔ cup all-purpose flour, plus 2 tablespoons

¼ teaspoon salt

3 cups pitted cherries (if using frozen, 2 12-ounce bags, thawed and drained)

Butter for the skillet

Preheat oven to 350°F.

Combine all ingredients except cherries and 2 tablespoons of the flour in a blender and blend on high for 1 minute. In a large bowl, toss the cherries and 2 tablespoons flour. Pour batter over cherries and mix.

Pour batter into buttered 9- or 10-inch cast-iron skillet. Bake 45 to 50 minutes, until a toothpick comes out clean. Dust with powdered sugar and serve immediately with a dollop of whipped cream.

CHOCOLATE SOUFFLÉ ▷

SERVES 6

There is no dessert more elite than the chocolate soufflé. It's so elite that waiters have to ask up front if you want it to be your end-of-meal treat, before you've even had a chance to dip into the bread basket and get a poppy seed caught in your front tooth. For such an uppity dish, it's surprisingly easy to make at home and rather inexpensive. This one is for you chocolate freaks.

6 ounces good-quality semi-sweet baking chocolate, chopped

2 tablespoons strong brewed coffee or espresso

1 teaspoon vanilla extract

Dash of cinnamon

3 egg yolks

6 egg whites (reserve 3 extra yolks to make pots de crème next weekend! See page 100)

Dash of salt

¼ cup sugar, plus extra for dusting

Butter for the baking dishes

In a metal or glass bowl fit snugly over a saucepan of gently simmering water, melt the chocolate, stirring frequently. Stir in the coffee, vanilla, and cinnamon. Remove the bowl and cool for a few minutes, then stir in the egg yolks.

With an electric mixer on medium-high, whip the egg whites with the salt until soft peaks start to form. Add sugar a little at a time, continuing to whip until stiff peaks form.

Stir 1 cup of the egg whites into the chocolate. Fold this mixture into the remaining whites. Spoon into a large soufflé dish or individual 6-ounce ramekins that have been buttered and dusted with sugar.

Bake on a cookie sheet for 18 to 20 minutes or until soufflé is puffed and crusty but center is jiggly. Dust with powdered sugar and serve immediately.

CREPES

MAKES A LOT

These thin, sexy little pancakes can be filled with anything from Nutella to jam to whipped cream. Because they're made with ingredients you probably already have around the house, they cost just pennies per crepe. I told you being fabulous doesn't have anything to do with money!

1 cup all-purpose flour

¾ cup milk

½ cup water

2 eggs

2 tablespoons sugar

2 tablespoons unsalted butter, melted

1 teaspoon vanilla extract

In a bowl, whisk all the ingredients together and refrigerate for at least 1 hour.

Grease a small skillet with butter and set over low heat. Using a ¼-cup measuring cup, add batter to the skillet and swirl to spread. Cook for 30 seconds and flip. Cook for another 10 to 15 seconds. Repeat.

Fill crepes with butter, sugar, chocolate sauce, jams, fruits, whipped cream.

Try topping with Bourbon Banana Sauce (page 86). For savory crepes, omit sugar and vanilla extract. Fill with everything from ham and cheese to Curried Chicken Salad (page 68) or Chicken Vol-au-Vent (page 78) and place in the broiler for 1 minute before serving.

CHEAP TRICK

Freeze leftover batter or finished crepes for your next gathering. If freezing finished crepes, layer wax paper between each one.

DESSERTS

GRILLED FRUIT ▷

Grilled fruit is easy, elegant, healthy, and thrifty. Please, make sure your grill grates are spotless, as charred pieces of salmon do not enhance the flavor of this recipe.

FOR THE GRILLED FRUIT
Your favorite fruits (peaches, plums, pineapples, bananas, apples, etc.)

Extra-virgin olive oil

FOR THE TOPPING
1 cup ricotta cheese

2 tablespoons honey

2 teaspoons cinnamon

1 teaspoon vanilla extract (almond extract is also delicious)

Dash of salt

Toasted nuts and fresh mint, roughly chopped, for garnish

FOR THE GRILLED FRUIT
Halve your fruit and lightly brush with olive oil. Grill for 2 to 3 minutes on each side.

FOR THE TOPPING
Combine the ricotta, honey, cinnamon, vanilla, and salt in a bowl. Add a dollop to each piece of fruit. Drizzle with more honey. Top with nuts and mint. You could also add a few drops of balsamic vinegar.
  Serve in bowls.

MIXED BERRY TRIFLE ▷

SERVES 8–10

Right now someone in the House of Windsor is digging into a trifle. You might not think to look to the British for dessert options, but trifle is always a hit at big parties. It's not overwhelming or heavy and it looks fabulous on the table. It's one of my signature desserts. Using fresh berries and store-bought lemon curd saves time and money.

FOR THE TRIFLE

2 pounds mixed fresh berries (raspberries, strawberries, blackberries)

½ cup sugar

1 package ladyfinger cookies

1 cup raspberry liqueur (such as Chambord)

One 10-ounce jar of lemon curd

Mint leaves and extra berries, for garnish

FOR THE WHIPPED CREAM

2 cups chilled heavy cream

1 teaspoon vanilla extract

4 tablespoons confectioners' sugar

FOR THE TRIFLE

Hull the strawberries. Rinse and drain the berries and cut the strawberries in half. In a medium-size bowl, mix the fresh berries with sugar. Line a shallow dish with the ladyfingers and splash with raspberry liqueur.

FOR THE WHIPPED CREAM

In a chilled bowl, using a handheld or stand mixer on medium speed (and the whisk beater, if it has one), whip the heavy cream and vanilla until it begins to thicken, about 1 minute. Slowly add sugar and continue whipping until soft peaks form, another 2 to 3 minutes.

Layer the trifle bowl first with ladyfingers, then lemon curd, then berries, and repeat layering. Top with whipped cream. Garnish with mint and extra berries.

CHEAP TRICK

If you don't have raspberry liqueur, use any other strong liquor, such as brandy or cognac.

DESSERTS

STRAWBERRY NAPOLEONS ▷

SERVES 6–8

I've never had a Napoleon complex, probably because I'm six foot four, but I can't resist a napoleon—layers of sweet custard alternating with crispy deliciousness. Plus, I just like the way they look with that stripe down the middle. I used to always think, "I could never make a napoleon. It's too fancy for me." But you know what? Nothing's too fancy for me! And nothing's too fancy for you!

FOR THE PASTRY CREAM

3 cups whole milk or half-and-half

1 teaspoon vanilla extract

Pinch of salt

8 large egg yolks

1¼ cups sugar

¼ cup all-purpose flour

FOR THE ICING

1 cup confectioners' sugar

½ teaspoon vanilla extract

3 teaspoons milk

FOR THE NAPOLEONS

30 graham crackers

1 ounce semi-sweet chocolate, melted

One 10-ounce package strawberries, hulled and sliced lengthwise

FOR THE PASTRY CREAM

In a deep saucepan over medium-high heat, add the milk, vanilla, and salt. Stir and bring to a boil.

Meanwhile, in a large bowl, using an electric mixer on low, mix egg yolks and sugar until smooth and thick. Gradually mix in the flour.

Pour the hot milk into the egg mixture one ladle at a time, whisking each time. Pour the mixture back into the pot and cook over medium heat, whisking constantly, until the mixture comes to a boil and thickens, about 7 to 8 minutes. Let boil for 30 seconds.

Set a strainer over a stainless-steel bowl and pour the pastry cream through it to remove any lumps.

Press a piece of plastic wrap over the surface of the bowl and refrigerate until cool.

FOR THE ICING

In a small mixing bowl, add the sugar and vanilla and stir in milk 1 teaspoon at a time to form a thick icing. If mixture becomes too runny, add more sugar.

FOR THE NAPOLEONS

In an 8-by-8-inch glass baking dish lined with aluminum foil, place a layer of graham crackers, a layer of chocolate, a layer of strawberries, a layer of pastry cream, and repeat. Finish with a layer of graham crackers. Frost with the icing.

Pour the melted chocolate into a plastic bag, snip the corner, and drizzle chocolate over the top in parallel rows. Run a toothpick back and forth through the chocolate to create the classic feather design.

SALTED CARAMEL POTS DE CRÈME

▷ MAKES 8

Everything you need to make these little cups of heaven is likely in your pantry now. This may be the most delicious pudding you will ever have.

¼ cup water

1 cup sugar

1¼ cups skim milk

1¼ cups cream

8 large egg yolks

Kosher salt

In a heavy saucepan, bring the water and sugar to a low boil over medium-high heat, stirring constantly, and cook for 8 to 10 minutes, until the mixture turns a deep golden brown or amber. When the sugar begins to caramelize and turn brown, it will become dark quickly, so keep an eye on it.

Meanwhile, combine the milk and cream in a saucepan and bring to a gentle simmer.

Remove the sugar from the heat and gradually stir in the milk and cream. The mixture will bubble. Return to the heat and cook until sugar dissolves and is thoroughly incorporated, about 5 minutes. Set aside to cool for 10 minutes.

Preheat oven to 325°F.

In a large bowl, preferably with a spout, whisk the egg yolks. Temper the eggs by adding caramel very gradually, until combined. Strain the mixture into a 4-cup measuring cup.

Divide the custard among eight 6-ounce ramekins. Set ramekins in a roasting pan lined with a dish towel. Pour boiling water until it reaches 1 inch up the sides of the roasting pan. Bake until the edges of the custards are set but the center is still jiggly, about 40 minutes. Set the roasting pan on a rack to cool. Sprinkle with kosher salt and chill for several hours or overnight.

CHEAP TRICK

Freeze the leftover egg whites and make chocolate soufflé (see page 90) next weekend! Or make an egg-white omelet for breakfast tomorrow. Haven't you had enough cholesterol this week?

DESSERTS

cocktails

It should come as no surprise to anyone that I like the sauce, but I'm actually not a boozehound. IT'S TRUE! While I love a good cocktail, I don't enjoy making stupid decisions under the influence, like the ones I made in the mid-'90s. So do me a favor and drink responsibly. I don't want to see you on the corner of some tabloid with candle wax on your nipples and a "little person" riding you piggyback. Ah, memories.

BOURBON RICKEY ▷———————————————

MAKES 1 COCKTAIL

2 ounces bourbon

Juice of ½ lime

1 teaspoon sugar

Seltzer

Lime wedge

In a shaker filled with ice, add the bourbon, lime juice, and sugar. Shake well and pour into a lowball glass filled with ice. Top with seltzer and garnish with a lime wedge.

CHAMPAGNE SORBET COCKTAIL

MAKES 1 COCKTAIL

1 scoop sorbet

4 ounces sparkling wine or
champagne

Add a scoop of your favorite sorbet to a champagne
glass and fill with sparkling wine or champagne.

CUCUMBER-LIME GIN AND TONIC ▷——————————

MAKES 1 COCKTAIL

2 slices seedless cucumber, plus 1 spear for garnish

1 lime round

2 ounces gin

4 ounces tonic

Mint leaves for garnish

Lime wedge

In a tall glass, add cucumber and lime and muddle. Add gin and ice, then tonic, and stir to combine. Garnish with mint, cucumber spear, and lime wedge.

1 bottle inexpensive Spanish red wine, such as a tempranillo or rioja

1½ cups brandy

½ cup fresh squeezed orange juice, oranges reserved

¼ cup fresh lemon juice, lemons reserved

1 cup sugar

Rounds of orange, lemon, or lime for garnish

In a blender, combine the wine, brandy, orange juice, lemon juice, and sugar. Fill the blender with ice and blend on high until combined. Serve in glasses garnished with a slice of orange, lemon, or lime.

To make Sangría without ice, mix ingredients in a pitcher and chop the reserved lemons and oranges into small cubes, add to pitcher, and chill. Serve in wineglasses filled with ice.

Stretch it a little further for a party by topping each glass with lemon-lime soda.

KIR

MAKES 1 COCKTAIL

1 ounce crème de cassis

4 ounces chilled white wine

Lemon twist

In a wineglass, add crème de cassis and wine. Stir to combine and garnish with a lemon twist. To make a Kir Royale, substitute sparkling wine for the white wine.

TEQUILA SUNRISE

MAKES 1 COCKTAIL

1½ ounces white tequila

1 ounce crème de cassis or grenadine

Lime juice

Seltzer

Lime wedge

Fill a tall glass with ice and add the tequila, crème de cassis, and lime juice. Top with seltzer and garnish with a lime wedge.

OLD-FASHIONED

MAKES 1 COCKTAIL

1 orange round
Maraschino cherry
1 teaspoon sugar
Splash of water
2 ounces bourbon
3 dashes bitters

In a shaker or tall mixing glass, add the orange round, maraschino cherry, sugar, and splash of water and muddle. Add bourbon and bitters, mix and pour into an old-fashioned glass with or without ice.

POMEGRANATE COSMO

MAKES 1 COCKTAIL

3 ounces vodka

1 ounce Cointreau or other orange-flavored liqueur

1 ounce pomegranate juice

Lemon twist

In a shaker filled with ice, add the vodka, Cointreau, pomegranate juice, and shake well. Pour into a chilled martini glass and serve with a lemon twist.

3 ounces brandy or cognac

1 ounce Cointreau or other orange-flavored liqueur

½ ounce lemon juice

Sugar for the rim

1 orange round

1 lemon round

In a shaker filled with ice, add the brandy or cognac, Cointreau, and lemon juice and shake well. Pour into a chilled martini glass rimmed with sugar. Garnish with orange and lemon rounds.

DÉCOR

(CRAFTS!)

SURROUND
YOURSELF
with
COLORS
that **FLATTER** you.

he men in my family are good at fixing motorcycles and welding I-beams together and building extensions on their houses. I like glitter. My dad can dissect a broken air conditioner and find fascination in repairing it, whereas I enjoy examining objets d'art and figuring out how to make similar ones at home.

I'm not so good with the butch things, but as it turns out, I'm pretty handy! I discovered this thanks to my obsession with mosaics. See, I used to travel to work in Manhattan on the subway (still do sometimes), and to avoid the gaze of weirdos and sociopaths, I would focus on the beautiful mosaics lining the stations. I became fascinated with the craftsmanship that went into these mosaics and had the itch to make my own. After completing an eight-week mosaic class, I ended up with a fabulous table and I've never looked back.

I guess you could call what I do "crafting," though the C-word, I must admit, tweaks me out a little, as it conjures images of women in crocheted vests and short, sensible haircuts. I like to craft while wearing something cute and drinking a crisp sauvignon blanc. That's how I recommend you craft too. None of this roll-out-of-bed-and-fall-into-a-basket-of-fabric-remnants crap. Treat your crafts with the respect they deserve. Put on a little lip gloss and some Tom Jones. You know, like you would for a third date. If your projects think you really care about them, they're more likely to put out.

When I told people I was writing this book, some had the nerve to say, "What the hell do you know about being on a budget?" To which I snapped, "You don't know my life!"

Sure, I've got some money now—not as much as Honey Boo Boo—but for many years I was broker than broke, to the tune of $87,000 in debt and making $24,000 a year. Good times. But I didn't want to be reminded every day that I was living hand-to-mouth, so I always kept my apartment looking somewhat upscale. And I did that by being clean, shopping wisely, and getting crafty. In this section you'll find some of the things I made when I was paying my dues (and my credit card bills) while living in New York City in the '90s.

But before we craft, we must **cleanse.** Here's my easy-peasy cheapo plan to make over your space in **FOUR STEPS.**

Step 1

SCOUR LIKE YOUR SOUL DEPENDS *on it!*

Let's say you want to make over your living room. The first thing you have to do is move every piece of furniture and every accessory the hell outta there. Now get down on your knees and scrub like there's no tomorrow. There's a brilliant scene in *American Beauty* you might want to use as motivation. If you haven't seen it, Annette Bening plays a high-strung real estate agent who's preparing to show a house and she is just cleaning like a madwoman and repeating her mantra, "I will sell this house today." Oh, it's genius. I *live* for her. Every time I attack the bathroom grout, I pretend I'm Annette. And let's keep that our little secret.

The cost of this step? Nada. Except maybe springing for some cleaning supplies. Microfiber cloths are pretty awesome and delightfully reusable. And a combination of white vinegar (1/2 cup), baking soda (1/4 cup), and water (one gallon) works wonders. Please don't ever mix bleach and ammonia—you'll die. Or give birth to kids with three eyes.

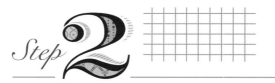

Step 2

GET *with the* PLAN, PAM!

Determine the purpose of your living room. How will you use it? For genteel conversation with your book club? As a rehearsal studio to act out your fantasy of being a Rockette? Spaces used for quiet contemplation can handle more furniture than ones used to entertain large extended families. I highly recommend taping out a floor plan to visualize furniture placement, using blue painter's tape that won't leave sticky residue. The scale of the room weighs heavily in selecting where things go. Just as a big-framed lady can wear big prints and carry a large handbag, a spacious room can handle an oversize sofa as well as bold wallpaper. But smaller rooms need smaller furniture—or less of it. It's all about creating the right proportions. You need about two feet of space around most pieces of furniture to create a good flow. Allow eighteen inches between a coffee table and a sofa or chairs. And for television viewing, allow six feet between the TV and the sofa. If you have too much stuff, find another place for it: in the attic or Mom's basement or a guest bedroom.

When you've got the blue tape on the floor, act out how you'll use the room. I do this all the time. It's fun! "Well, hello, Carol. Thank you for coming over today. Please have a seat on the chaise. Oh, I just realized you can't get to it without stepping on the buffet. Silly me."

Step 3

TIME *for a* WHOLE NEW HUE

Touching up moldings and painting the walls with a fresh coat of paint does wonders in refreshing the look and feel of your home. It's like wearing good foundation garments—you need a solid base in order to build fabulously up! Painting the walls is probably the fastest and easiest way to change the entire feeling of a room for a relatively small sum. As soon as the last coat goes on, you'll witness the transformation into a whole new space, fresh and clean as a summer's day. And, having painted more rooms than I care to count, I can give you these pieces of advice: Spackle the cracks, use fine-grade sandpaper to smooth out imperfections before you paint, do a coat of primer (even though you don't want to), and choose a color that you think might be too light. When you see a color on a paint chip that floats your boat, buy the paint that's a shade lighter. I have never said, "I wish this wall color were brighter!" But I have said many times, "I should have chosen a lighter shade. I'm such a dumb-ass."

COLOR
Is to DYE *For*

Choose colors wisely. But please: Choose color! Colors like "Wistful Wheat" and "Day on the Dunes" are just code words for beige. Boring, blah, blech.

The best colors are ones that make you happy and that you look good in. Here's a trick: Paint a swatch on the wall. Stand in front of it and have someone take a picture of you. Now examine. Does the color complement your skin tone or wash you out? And is it time for a mole check because that freckle on your clavicle is looking mighty large?

Just like you don't want a shirt to make you look drab, you don't want your main entertaining room to scream "sad sack." Look at that picture again. How does it make you feel? Cheery, regretful, irate? Colors elicit an emotional response, so selecting one that is right for you is a very individual choice. But for once in your life, don't play it safe. If you have always wanted to live inside a pumpkin, choose an autumnal orange, if only as an accent wall. You can always paint again if the hue on the wall makes you want to listen to songs by The Cure and cry all day.

Step 4

BE *a* RUTHLESS BITCH

Finally, don't put clutter back in the room. I just helped you clean it and now you plan to crap it all up again?! Don't make me come over there and whoop you upside the head.

With every accessory you bring back into the room, you must ask yourself, "Do I even LIKE this? Or am I putting it on the coffee table because Aunt Betty gave it to me on my sixteenth birthday while I was in my harlequin phase?" If it's chic, keep it. If it's not, chuck it. Don't let the past screw up your future fabulousness. And don't worry about hurting people's feelings! People shouldn't give you ugly stuff to begin with. It hurts my feelings when they do, and as we all know, my feelings are more important than anyone else's.

In case you were wondering, here's the difference between a collection and clutter: A "collection" is limited in number and cleverly displayed. "Clutter" is squeezing every last figurine you own on a shelf where they collect dust and make people talk about you behind your back. If you just *have to* display those jaunty plastic penguins you've amassed over the years, rotate them in and out of the living room. Even the best art museums change things up now and then. In my humble opinion, displaying more than six of anything at one time is creepy.

And so is any lifelike doll owned by anyone who has successfully exited puberty.

NOW WHAT?

Maybe you have a little extra cash to spend. Maybe the living room looks so enticing after the simple makeover that you just can't stop the wheel of fabulousness from turning. Add another layer to the room, my friend, with either or both of these enhancements.

FURNITURE

If you've already flipped ahead to the "Style" chapter, you know that I highly recommend visiting upscale stores to fondle and stare at expensive clothes. The same goes for furniture. I want to shout it from the rooftops: You can't look expensive if you don't know what expensive things look like! Same goes for your pad. So get out there and plop your cute tush down on some overpriced love seats. Visit high-end furniture stores to see what pricey pieces look and feel like. Furniture is expensive. No way around it. Is it easier to create a gorgeous room on a $100,000 budget? Hell, yeah. But if you know how to make smart choices, you can be *Freakin' Fabulous* for less. (I'd also like to take this opportunity to say that I've been to the homes of many rich people who have crappy taste, so money does certainly not guarantee fabulousness. I'd much rather spend time in a clean, uncluttered, freshly painted room than in one dominated by a 14-karat-gold statue of Venus de Milo riding a panther.)

When you're not shopping, buy decorating magazines and make a folder of the rooms that inspire you. That's what interior designers do. Bookmark the websites that get your creative juices flowing, or scour Pinterest for inspiration and start pinning your favorite looks. Once you develop the visual language of decorating, you can "speak" it when shopping at more affordable retailers.

And don't think you've got to get it all done at once. Add in furniture slowly. Pacing yourself will prevent errors in design judgment and ending up with a living room that looks sloppy and rushed.

Think SECONDHAND, *Not* SLOPPY SECONDS

Vintage furniture and knickknacks (in moderation) can add character to a room and help you save money. I like to have one vintage piece in every room because it seems to "ground it." You know, make it feel like the whole room didn't come out of some catalog. In 1995 I bought a pair of industrial steel dressers at a flea market—they were probably first used in some 1950s mental asylum—and I still have them in my bedroom. Sure, they have a few dings, but these days so do I. I call my flaws "character." Same goes for my furniture. Here's what to look for when shopping vintage:

1. Shop flea markets, estate sales, thrift stores, auctions, and yard sales. Things tend to get a bit pricey at antique and vintage outposts.

2. Turn the object over and over or give that piece of furniture the attention of a crime scene investigator. Are there stains, rips, wobbly knobs, too much wear and tear? Open all the drawers in that credenza and make sure they don't stick. If it is built solidly, not in terrible disrepair, and priced fairly (don't be embarrassed to haggle), it's probably a good buy. You're not looking to be a breakout star on the next season of *Antiques Roadshow*; you're just out to buy an affordable and lovely addition to your home.

3. Ask the dealer when the new merchandise arrives and if the outlet ever has sales.

4. Keep your paint colors and fabric swatches, as well as the dimensions and a sketch of the room you're redoing in your purse, man purse, or recycled tote. You will probably have to make an on-the-spot decision, so you need to be armed with all the important info.

5. Know what you can and can't do. Are you up for repainting that mauve dresser a vibrant cobalt? (Pretty easy.) Could you sand down that old wooden end table and put on a fresh stain? (Moderately difficult.) What about replacing ugly drawer pulls? (Piece of cake.) Or reupholstering a sofa? (Save that for the professionals!) Knowing your refurbishing talents—or what you're at least willing to attempt—will help you determine if a certain piece is right for your home.

 y this point, you get it— *being fabulous doesn't have to cost a lot.* Employing the power of the craft saves money, gives you one-of-a-kind original style, and provides an outlet for your creativity that you haven't enjoyed since that interpretive dance class in college. Ah-hem.

When your friends exclaim that your fabulous décor must have cost you a fortune, remember to take the compliment and shut your trap! Smile, nod politely, and simply say, "Thank You." Practice in the mirror.

An easy place to start decorating with crafts is on your table. When I'm dressing up my table I like to mix it up, from the plates to the napkins, like I did here.

I mix china that I found at flea markets, vintage finds from the Internet with some of my grandma's old china, or something new. It looks chic as long as the colors and patterns work together.

The same goes for table linens and napkins. And when it comes to accents, it's okay to mix your metallics.

See how all of those concepts are working here on this table. Guess what? I made the table runner, napkins, napkin rings, votives, and vases myself. You're impressed.

Right now, I'm smiling, nodding politely, and saying "Thank you."

And, I'm going to show you how to do it too.

CLINTON'S
THERAPY COUCH

"I just cannot rid myself of my guilty feelings. My mother-in-law gives me these expensive china figurines that I do not want! I know you think I should donate them to charity or throw them in the attic, but I would feel terrible if she came over and noticed that they weren't displayed. What should I do?"

Look, guilt is an emotion I'm very familiar with, but you should never feel guilty in your own home about something you didn't even want there! This kind of thing is always about communication. You *must* have a conversation with your mother-in-law, whether you want to or not. Figure out how to have a little alone time with her and say, "Mom, you know I just adore you and our relationship is so special to me, but these figurines don't really go with the decorating scheme Jim and I have decided to try. I will always treasure the ones you've already given us, but you don't have to buy us any more. I hope this doesn't hurt your feelings. Let's go have a drink; I know how much you like the sauce."

A WORD *on* FLOWERS

Flowers are a lovely way to add beauty to any table. Remember, though, that the point of your dinner party is to allow your guests to gossip about everyone who didn't show up, and they can't do that if they can't see one another. Keep your flowers low on the table so that your guests can see everyone and the food.

You don't have to break the bank on flowers. These can be inexpensive white carnations and spider mums. I can hear you gasping in horror now: "Carnations! Clinton, not you!" Yes, me. Don't they look fabulous? Cut low and arranged tightly, they're elegant and clean.

Keep thinking outside the box. I'm not a fan of those infamous floral fillers—ferns and baby's breath. Instead, herbs such as rosemary and mint make a chic substitute.

Note:
We cut 19-by-19-inch
squares to make 18-by-18-inch
napkins, but the size of your napkin
is a matter of personal preference
and depends on the size of the shirt
you are using. As a general rule,
cut the square 1 inch larger
in length and width than
the size of the finished
napkin.

NAPKINS MADE FROM SHIRTS?

What?

Yellowed armpits and a wine stain down the front of your favorite shirt? It happens to the best of us. Well, it's time to say good-bye to those suckers. (Even the thrift store doesn't want them. They have standards!) I raided my own closet to make these superchic serviettes. Seriously! You may even have seen me sporting some of these prints on *What Not to Wear*! Speaking of prints, don't worry about matching. A table can be great fun when it doesn't look all prissy. Make sure you wash the shirts in hot water, and don't use the underarm parts!

napkins method

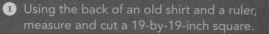

MATERIALS:
old shirts, ruler, scissors, iron, ironing board, hem tape

1. Using the back of an old shirt and a ruler, measure and cut a 19-by-19-inch square.

2. Crease a ¼-inch hem around the entire square and iron.

3. Fold this hem over a piece of ¼-inch hem tape and iron again.

4. Trim away excess hem tape and fold.

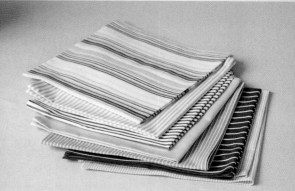

JAZZY JEWELRY NAPKIN RINGS

You can't swing a rubber chicken through a flea market without hitting a box o' brooches, and that's where I found these beauties. It's pretty rare that a woman will wear a brooch these days (I am making a sad face), but these sparkly nuggets shouldn't go to waste. Great-Aunt Sally will be so happy you put her best jewelry to good use, she'll be doing backflips in her grave! Once again, don't worry about matching. Mix those metallics and add some shine to your tabletop.

napkin rings method

Note: You can wrap the ribbon as many times as you like; more wraps makes a stiffer napkin ring. Two times around would be the minimum.

MATERIALS: ribbon, fabric stiffener, plastic wrap, paper towel tube, thrift store pins

1. Begin by dragging the ribbon through fabric stiffener. Remove excess with your fingers.

2. Wrap plastic wrap around the paper towel tube, then wrap ribbon around the tube twice.

3. Allow to dry for at least twenty-four hours, remove from tube, and pin thrift store jewelry through ribbon.

127

Note:

Yardage and fabric are
dependent on the size of your table.
As a general rule, measure how
wide you would like the table runner
to be on your table and divide that
number by 3. Add 1 inch, and that
is the dimension of each patchwork
square. (For example, we wanted
our runner to be 24 inches wide:
24 ÷ 3 = 8 + 1 = 9.
So our cut squares were
9 by 9 inches.)

COLOR-BLOCKED TABLE RUNNER

A table runner is the easiest way in the world to bring color, texture, and pattern to your dining space. When an entire tablecloth feels too fancy, a runner is the perfect alternative. Remember, you eat with your eyes—so even if you burnt the hell out of dinner, it will taste delicious when it's sitting on this.

color-blocked table runner method

MATERIALS: scissors, fabric, pins, sewing machine, thread, iron, ironing board

1. Cut fabric into 9-by-9-inch squares, pin and sew together in sets of 3, using a ½-inch seam allowance.

2. Iron seams open and flat.

3. Pin and sew together sets of 3 along the long edges until you have reached the desired length for the runner.

4. Iron your table runner and display on the table.

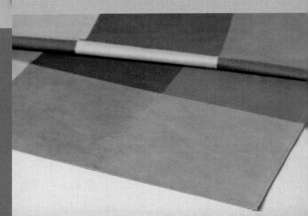

Hot Tip

To remove wax quickly from a votive holder, place in the freezer for half an hour and pop out the old wax.

REHABILITATED VA-VA-VOTIVES AND VA-VA-VASES

This is your lucky day. When my television career has dried up, I'll be making and selling these out on the corner in front of my building for twenty bucks a pop. But I'm giving them to you for free! This craft takes something so inexpensive and makes it look so expensive that you'd be crazy not to do it. By the way, I would never set a table without candles because everybody looks better in candlelight. That's how half the babies in America were made. True fact. Look it up.

rehabilitated votives method

MATERIALS:
masking tape, electrical tape, old votive holders and vases, painter's tape, old cardboard box, silver metallic spray paint, candles

1. Use masking or electrical tape to mark off areas to be painted on the votive.
2. Cover the rest in painter's tape. Remove masking or electrical tape and leave painter's tape intact.
3. Working outside or in a well-ventilated area, set the votive on a surface protected by an old cardboard box and spray it with metallic spray paint.
4. Allow to dry and remove the painter's tape. Alternatively, use several light coats of the metallic spray paint, allowing time to dry in between, instead of one heavy coat (to prevent runny paint).
5. Place candles in votives or add flowers and use them as a vase. Display.

I FREAKIN' LOVE MERCURY GLASS!

This lamp is being sold for big bucks in the catalog sitting next to your toilet bowl. Enough said. You can also use this trendy technique on anything made of glass—vases, old jars, mirrors, holiday ornaments!

mercury glass lamp method

MATERIALS: painter's tape, glass lamp base, old cardboard box, spray bottle, vinegar, water, "looking glass" spray paint, paper towels

Note:
Wax can be poured to ¼ to ½ inches below the rim of the cup.

Hot Tip

The spray bottle should be on the finest-mist setting. You can repeat the process as many times as necessary to get the desired effect.

1 Using painter's tape, tape off everything but the glass base of the lamp—including hardware, connector, and wires. In a well-ventilated area, or working outside, set lamp inside an old cardboard box. Using spray bottle, spray liberally with a 1:1 solution of vinegar and water.

2 Immediately spray with spray paint. Let spray paint dry for 1 to 2 minutes, then spray again with vinegar solution and dry for 3 to 5 more minutes. Using paper towels, gently blot away excess moisture. Do not rub. This gives the mottled mercury glass effect.

3 Allow to dry, remove protective tape, add lampshade, and display.

Hot Tip

If the wax sinks in the center when cooled, poke a few holes around wick with a knife or pin and add an additional small amount of melted wax to center.

NOT-JUST-FOR-TEA-ANYMORE TEACUP CANDLES

We all have one: a set of china that's been passed down through the generations. And though it's a pattern we never would have chosen and doesn't match anything in our home, it's kind of precious and sentimental. Maybe all you have left is a few old teacups. Or maybe that's all your grandmother thought you were responsible enough to handle. But you and I both know that deep down, you didn't want those teacups anyway—you wanted money. Well, show that old biddy how much you didn't need her inheritance by making these candles! (I should stop writing this book while drinking gin.)

teacup candles method

MATERIALS: paraffin wax, 2-cup glass measuring cup, 2-quart saucepan, wicks, old teacups, chopsticks

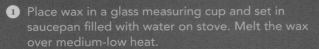

1. Place wax in a glass measuring cup and set in saucepan filled with water on stove. Melt the wax over medium-low heat.

2. Once the wax is melted, place a wick inside each teacup. Using caution, because the wax is hot, pour the wax into the cup.

3. If the wick shifts, reposition and stabilize with the chopstick.

4. Allow to cool. Display.

135

People say to buy art if it speaks to you. I agree, as long as your art doesn't whisper "Redrum" into your ear at night. For crying out loud, buy the stuff that makes you smile and don't worry too much about what other people will think. You kind of can't win. I will not like some of your art. You will not like some of my art. Who cares? I don't live in your house and your restraining order prevents you from entering mine.

CLINTON KELLY FREAKIN' FABULOUS

SHADY CHIC

Can't seem to part with your favorite lamp but the shade is all yellowed and busted like a meth-head's teeth? Make this.

lampshade method

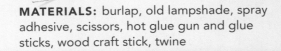

MATERIALS: burlap, old lampshade, spray adhesive, scissors, hot glue gun and glue sticks, wood craft stick, twine

① Spread burlap on a flat surface. Coat the lampshade with spray adhesive and roll across burlap to cover. Let the ends of the burlap overlap the shade by 1 to 2 inches.

② Trim excess burlap from top and bottom of lampshade, leaving a border 1 to 2 inches.

③ Using a hot glue gun and wooden craft stick, glue the excess burlap border to the inside of the lamp. Press edge with craft stick as you glue. Trim excess.

④ To finish the edges, glue twine over the rough, inside edges of the burlap using the hot glue gun. Display.

TERRARIUMS!

They're awesome!

My passion for terrariums originated with an orphaned newt in the '70s. Along with Dorothy Hamill haircuts and "The Hustle," terrariums were kind of a big deal in that decade. When I was six, I found a newt and let it live in our terrarium. So maybe the newt was more newt-napped than orphaned, but I soon felt bad for the little guy. He looked so sad despite his chic new home, so I put him back in the great outdoors. But terrariums still hold a special place in my heart.

Aside from providing temporary shelter for small creatures, terrariums add life to a room, but can run up to $200 in home furnishing stores. My version will set you back a fraction of that. Even if you've killed every plant in your life, succulents are pretty hard to destroy. The layering adds great texture and a little bit of pattern to a room. Everyone should have at least one living, breathing thing in their house. Sorry, your husband doesn't count.

decorative terrarium method

MATERIALS:
soil, sand,
mason jar,
succulent plants,
moss, stones

1. Begin by adding alternating layers of soil and sand to the jar.
2. Continue adding soil and sand, pressing firmly after each layer, until layers are about halfway up the jar.
3. Now add plants, moss, and stones, and display. *Spend all that money you saved on a new pair of shoes!*

IDIOT-PROOF ART!

Last summer, I was soaking up the sun on a bamboo mat while sipping cocktails on the pebbly shores of the Côte d'Azur, when I was struck with this design inspiration. Okay, that didn't happen, but it sounds like something that could have happened to a *Freakin' Fabulous* guy like myself. In any case, it's what you should tell people when they compliment you up and down on how super fabulous this little piece of Mondrian-inspired art is.

bamboo mat art method

MATERIALS: bamboo mat, paint, painter's tape

1. Begin by painting the mat in one base color. Allow to dry.

2. Affix painter's tape to mat to block off your design.

3. Paint squares in different colors and allow to dry.

4. Remove tape and display. Hang where all of your friends and family can see and comment on your limitless talent.

THE MOST AMAZING WALL OF ART

When you're on a budget, it's hard to fill your home with art. Art is expensive! And I think that what artists do is really valuable, so it doesn't ruffle my feathers when original works cost big bucks. But if you can give up watching football or picking your toenails for one afternoon, and put that time and effort into creating something aside from a pile of toenails, you can make *Freakin' Fabulous* art.

I adore the idea of an entire wall of mismatched but coordinated art. Choose: (1) a color scheme, (2) common shapes, and (3) a common theme. Here, I selected a blue-green color scheme, round and oval shapes, and an outdoorsy theme. Most any theme will work—dogs, buildings, flowers, whatever you're into.

Then mix it up. Start with a few medallions that you can find in various shapes and sizes in home improvement stores. They cost from $4 to $50. Add some decoupage plates. These were less than $1 each! Decoupage is also a great way to use an old set of dishes. You're not limited to pressed flowers here. Anything can supply your design element, from photos to magazine images to paper to fabric. Next try an update on a childhood classic: silhouettes. Use images of objects or family members by taking silhouette snapshots, scanning and enlarging them on the computer, then printing and tracing. In a grouping they all sort of come together and they look happy. I love it! Whee!

painted ceiling medallions method

MATERIALS: old cardboard box, ceiling medallions, spray paint

1. Working outside or in a well-ventilated area, set the ceiling medallions on a surface protected by an old cardboard box and spray them with spray paint.

2. Allow to dry, then hang on your wall.

143

silhouettes method

MATERIALS: picture images, computer paper, stapler, craft knife or scissors, spray adhesive, construction or wrapping paper, painter's tape, frames, paint

1. Begin by placing an image on a plain piece of paper—staple around (not within) the image to hold it in place. Cut out your chosen image with a craft knife or scissors.

2. Spray the back of the image with spray adhesive and affix to colored construction or wrapping paper. Repeat as desired.

3. Once dry, trim paper to fit frame and assemble. Using painter's tape to protect glass, paint the frame with acrylic or latex paint to match your décor, if desired. Display.

decoupage plates method

MATERIALS: Mod Podge, clear glass plate, foam brush, pressed flowers and ferns, white plate, plate hanger

1. Working on a protected surface, apply Mod Podge to the back of the clear plate with a foam brush to avoid a brushstroke texture.

2. Place pressed flowers and ferns onto the wet Mod Podge.

3. Once all the flowers have been placed, carefully add another layer of Mod Podge over the flowers and ferns.

4. Allow to dry for at least 24 hours—then place a second, opaque white plate behind it. Hang the plates together on the wall with a plate hanger. Gaze at the gorgeousness you've created.

Hot Tip

HOW TO PRESS FLOWERS AND FERNS

Choose flowers and trim away most of the stems and leaves, and remove interior petals from large flowers like roses, then gently flatten with fingers. Place flowers in a folded piece of paper or tissue. Using a large, heavy book like a dictionary, sandwich the flowers between the pages and close the book. Choose a book you are okay with staining—the flowers may leak. Stack additional books on top to add weight. Allow to dry for at least one week.

145

BAMBOO SCREEN

I'm a fan of wallpaper, and dammit, I'm not ashamed to admit it! Not 1980s flocked wallpaper, but gorgeous, expensive-looking wallpaper. If you live in a rental apartment, you might not be allowed to paper the walls. Or you might have commitment issues. Whatever. This is a nice option for adding a beautiful print to your space. And you can take it with you when you move!

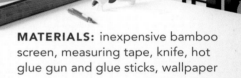

MATERIALS: inexpensive bamboo screen, measuring tape, knife, hot glue gun and glue sticks, wallpaper

bamboo screen method

1. Measure the panels of your bamboo screen. Using a knife, cut panels of wallpaper to size. Use a hot glue gun to carefully apply glue in lines along the inside of the panels. Press the wallpaper to the glue.

2. Repeat to cover all three panels. Pretty freakin' awesome, huh?

EGLOMISE?
What the heck is that?

Eglomise. I can never remember that word! I always want to say *vichyssoise* or *Égoïste*, the name of the cologne I wore in my senior year of college. Whatever you call it, eglomise (églomisé) is a really fun technique that produces instant art. If you screw it up, just rinse the paint right off and start over again. My inspiration for this tabletop is from a painting that I have in my apartment, which I found at an art fair. It was kind of expensive, and I looked at it, and I thought, "I could do that!" So I did! In fact, I used the eglomise technique twice here—on the tabletop and the tray—and I made that rug too! Remember I said don't be afraid of color. Well, I put my money where my mouth is, honey. One of my favorite color combinations is pink and purple, and I love the way they work together in this room.

MATERIALS: coffee table, custom-cut glass, electrical tape, paint, paintbrush

Note:
To keep from getting confused, you can make your spacer tape slightly shorter or use a different color electrical tape. Or stop drinking and crafting!

eglomise tabletop method

1. Measure your coffee table and have glass custom-cut to fit the top.

2. Begin by marking off design with electrical tape. To make even stripes, place one piece of electrical tape along one edge. Place another piece of electrical tape exactly parallel and right up against the first piece as a "spacer." Align another strip of electrical tape from one end of the glass to the other, along the spacer. Move the spacer to the other side of the last strip and continue to add strips of electrical tape, using the spacer in between.

3. Cover the cut edges of the glass with more electrical tape and paint the exposed glass. Allow to dry. Repeat.

4. Remove electrical tape, let glass dry at least 24 hours, then place painted side down on top of the coffee table. Display your custom table with pride.

MORE EGLOMISE!

Because I can't get enough.

An inexpensive picture frame can easily be turned into a chic serving tray for appetizers or cocktails using the same technique I used on the glass tabletop. (The frame might not be sturdy enough to carry around with drinks on it, so set it down first and put things on it. Learned that the hard way.)

eglomise serving tray method

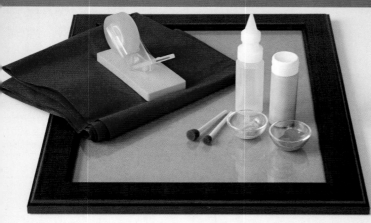

MATERIALS: picture frames, small round sponge brush, paints (one dark, one lighter, and a metallic), squeeze bottle, water, double-sided tape, tissue or wrapping paper

1. Carefully place the glass on a protected surface and, using the sponge brush, dot the glass with the darkest paint in a spiral pattern.

2. In a small squeeze bottle, mix a lighter paint with water in a 1:1 ratio. Shake well. Hold the squeeze bottle straight up and down and drip paint over the darker paint dots to cover.

3. Finish by adding accent dots in metallic paint.

4. Allow to dry. Using double-sided tape, affix the tissue or wrapping paper as backing and reassemble in picture frame . . . and go make some drinks!

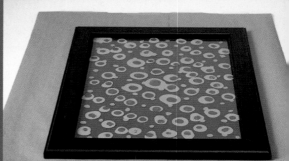

Hot Tip

Decorative or solid card stock or heavy paper can be cut to the size of the glass and placed between the glass and backing when framing. Alternatively, "wrap" the backing with tissue/wrapping paper—like a gift—before assembling the frame.

NICE RUG!

I know somebody out there is thinking, "I wish I could find a rug that looked like this." My reply: "Eh, let's just make it." Ombre, or graduated color, is a big statement in clothing, home accessories, even hair. I used it here to turn this boring off-white rug into a whimsical décor statement.

dip-dye rug method

MATERIALS:
fabric dye, water, large bucket, wool or cotton rug

1. Make a mixture of 2 tablespoons liquid dye per 4 quarts of water (or approximately 4 liters) in a large bucket or bin and fill until the level is about half as deep as you would like to dip the rug. Mix more dye bath if necessary. (If a solid, not ombre, effect is desired, make the dye bath level as deep as you would like to dip the rug.)

2. Place one side of rug in bucket and soak for about 15 minutes or until desired shade is reached. Remember that once the dye is rinsed and the rug is dry, the color will be several shades lighter.

3. Rinse excess dye from the rug, rinsing from the center of the rug outward, and hang, dyed side down, to dry. Place an old towel or paper towels under the rug to collect drips. Once the rug is mostly dry, repeat on the other side.

4. Next, to achieve your ombre effect, double the water in the bath but not the dye, dip each side again for 15 minutes, rinsing, hanging, and allowing time to dry in between. Allow to dry fully and display . . . and let the compliments come rolling in.

TURN YOUR VASE INTO A VAAHZ

You know all those blah glass vases that come with floral arrangements? Don't trash them. Turn them into little treasures.

dip-dye vases method

MATERIALS:
paint, string, old florist vases, container

1. Begin by pouring paint into a deep container. Tie a string around the neck of each vase and dip each vase on an angle into the paint. Hang the vase over a protected surface to dry.

2. Once the vases have dried, fill with your favorite flowers and display . . . and bask in the beauty of your VAAHZ.

Hot Tip

Be sure to tie the string around the neck of the vase FIRST (before dipping). Use the string to hang the vase to dry from a ladder, chair, etc. Place a piece of cardboard under the vase while drying to collect paint drips.

LARGE-FORMAT ART—FOR CHEAP!

If you frequent expensive hotels with all the dough you've saved by following my advice in this book, notice what's going on with the walls. Hotels can't put a piece of original artwork on every wall. It's too expensive, and rowdy patrons may try to stash it in their carry-on luggage upon checkout. Instead of taking this risk, smarty-pants hotel interior designers just frame beautiful pieces of fabric or wallpaper.

To buy large-scale art is very often cost-prohibitive. I'm talking thousands of dollars. And the truth of the matter is, beautiful art is accessible to us almost every day. Fabric and wallpaper is artwork for the masses and it's affordable. Real-life artists create the patterns! Now, go find a beautiful piece of fabric that you love, and take charge of your décor!

The custom frame is just the molding usually found along the floors and ceilings of homes. Seven feet of basic molding like we've used here costs six or seven dollars at home improvement stores.

large-format art method

MATERIALS:
fabric or wallpaper, measuring tape, scissors, level, pencil, molding, staple gun, hammer, nails, miter saw

1. Begin by choosing the area on your wall you want to cover, then measure and cut the fabric accordingly. Using a level and pencil, mark off where the fabric should be affixed. Using a staple gun or hammer and nails, affix the fabric to the wall. It is easiest to affix the top edge of the fabric first, then align the sides and bottom accordingly.

2. Measure and cut the molding into four pieces with a miter saw, so the edges are diagonal and will fit together in a frame around the fabric. Using a level, place the molding onto the wall so it covers the raw edge of the fabric. Nail the molding to the wall. Wow! Wow! Wow!

KEEPING IT NATURAL

I like natural touches in the house because I feel like they warm a place up, rather than giving off a cold and sterile vibe like a urologist's office. Just like that old Burt Bacharach song instructs, "Make this house into a home!" Here I used some of my favorite things: corn husks, gourds, pinecones, and nuts. It's perfect for a fall holiday display or just any old time, really.

CORN HUSK VOTIVES— Whee!

You can't get any less expensive than corn husks. It's a great way to add pizzazz and texture to an already bright flame.

corn husk votives method

MATERIALS:
corn husks,
scissors,
double-sided
tape or hot glue
gun and glue sticks,
glass votives, twine,
votive candles

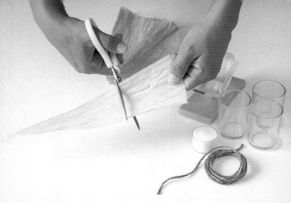

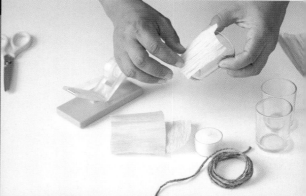

1. Begin by trimming the corn husks into pieces that are ¼ to ½ inch taller than the outside of the votive.

2. Affix double-sided tape to bottom of votive. A hot glue gun will also work.

3. Place corn husks onto tape to hold them in place temporarily.

4. Tie with a piece of twine.

5. Display with other votives on your mantel or holiday table.

Note:
Please do not leave your corn husk votives unattended. A table on fire is not fabulous unless a Benihana chef is also flipping shrimp into your mouth.

Hot Tip

I used a gloss-finish spray paint; if you like extra work you can also choose your favorite color of paint or spray paint, let it dry, and then apply a clear spray gloss finish.

GOT GOURDS?

I'm drawn to modernist, minimalist furniture, but I don't want a room that's filled with right angles and hard lines. Enter gourds. They have amorphous shapes and bumpy textures that add an unexpected twist to an otherwise modern aesthetic. Mine are all black, but you can paint them in different shades of the same color to create depth and interest.

gourds method

MATERIALS:
old cardboard box,
dried gourds, spray paint

Hot Tip

Do you have a cool, well-ventilated space inside or outside your home? Do you have a month to sit and wait? If you answered YES! to both questions, then you can dry some gourds. Since gourds are mostly water, you might see some mold start to form. Scrape it off with a butter knife and wipe the gourd. If a soft spot forms, throw the gourd away. It's rotting from the inside out.

· Ick.

1. Working outside or in a well-ventilated area, set the gourds on a surface protected by an old cardboard box and spray them with spray paint.
2. Allow to dry and display.

161

GLITZY CONES AND SNAZZY NUTS

Nothing says party time like shine, shine, shine! It's the same thing with an outfit. People always ask me, "What should I wear New Year's Eve?" And I always say, "Something shiny."

Pinecones bring the outdoors in and add a nice seasonal touch during fall and winter. But why have a pile of brown pinecones sitting around when you can have *Freakin' Fabulous* metallic ones? They are soooooo much better than the prescented potpourri kind sold in the supermarket—those things will look awful in your house . . . trust me. Nothing unfabulouses a room like a waft of cheap potpourri. It always makes me feel like the home owner is trying to mask the scent of a Number Two.

glitzy cones and snazzy nuts method

MATERIALS:
metallic spray paints, pinecones and nuts, spray adhesive, plastic bags, glitter

Metallic nuts are really chic. I adore them. Please don't eat them.

1. For simple spray-painted nuts and pinecones, follow the method for gourds.

2. To make glitzy nuts and pinecones, begin by spraying nuts or pinecones with spray adhesive. Place the nuts and pinecones in a plastic bag filled with glitter. Shake well to coat.

3. Allow to dry and display. Instant glitz and glamour!

PAINT YER BALLS!

These ornaments were one of my most popular crafts on *The Chew* last year. And they're so easy and inexpensive to make. You just get glass ornaments and pour paint into them and swirl them around a little bit. You don't even have to put them on the tree. Just put them in a beautiful bowl to bring some color and holiday spirit into the room. The same thing goes for the pine tree forms. I'm not big on literal symbolism. My house doesn't need to be swathed in red and green with Santa figurines on display for me to know it's that time of year. It's too obvious. These ornaments and tree forms are simple, dramatic, and elegant. I love them.

ball ornaments method

MATERIALS:
clear glass
ornaments,
water-based
glaze paint,
paints,
plastic cups

1. Remove the top of the ornament and add a small amount of glaze, about the size of a nickel, to the bottom.
2. Add generous drops of colored paints to the glaze.
3. Swirl the paints to cover the inside of the glass ball and create a pattern.
4. Turn the ball upside down and place in a plastic cup, allowing the excess paint to drain from the ornaments. Allow to dry overnight.
5. Replace the ornament tops and display in bowls or on tree.

164

Hot Tip

If paint drains from the ornament instead of adhering to the sides, use less glaze. Please know that this is not an exact science; it's crafts! Also, it's okay to add more paint or glaze if you need to. You can turn the ball (on its side, right-side up, etc.) in the plastic cup at intervals while it's drying to allow the paint to distribute evenly. Also, if you don't like how your ball turned out, you can wash it out with soapy water and start again, as long as the paint hasn't completely hardened (which generally happens after a few days).

LET'S GET CONICAL

A 12-inch Styrofoam cone costs about $3. Need I say more? Experiment with different fabrics, patterns, colors, and design elements to make a unique winter display.

tree forms method

MATERIALS:
conical Styrofoam forms, white computer paper, double-sided tape, dupioni silk fabric, pins, scissors, hot glue gun and glue sticks, black felt

1. Begin by wrapping the top of the Styrofoam form with a piece of regular computer paper to give it a pointed top. Affix with double-sided tape.

2. Iron your fabric and spread it on a flat surface. Pin one edge of the fabric to the tree form before rolling to make it easier. Roll up the tree form in the fabric and pin the fabric to the form.

3. Trim away excess fabric at the bottom, but leave a 2-inch border. Making a series of small cuts in the border, trim excess into small tabs. Using a hot glue gun, glue the tabs to the bottom of the tree form. Cut a circle of black felt to match the bottom of the tree and glue to cover.

4. Display with metallic balls and other Christmas delights.

STYLE

The WAY YOU **DRESS** TELLS **THE REST** of the WORLD HOW *you* EXPECT to be **TREATED.**

**E**ven after ten years and hundreds of episodes of *What Not to Wear*, it never ceases to amaze me how a style overhaul can change a woman's life.

It basically boils down to this: The way you dress tells the rest of the world how you expect to be treated. And when you are treated the way you really want to be treated, it feels pretty freakin' good.

Let's just take a minute to expand on that thought. (I'll use the example of a hooker, because who doesn't love a good hooker reference!) If you dress like a hooker, you're basically telling everyone around you, nonverbally, that you're comfortable being sexually objectified. And so, men might offer you money to perform various sexual acts. There may or may not be a problem with that. If you are indeed a hooker, your marketing strategy is perfectly aligned with your brand identity. Congrats! But if you're not actually a hooker, you've got a problem.

I'll give you another example: Let's say you dress like a complete and total slob—pajamas in public, an oversize hoodie, ratty hair thrown back in a scrunchie. How might this affect your day? Your boss might see you in the supermarket and make a mental note that you're not management material. A cute, available, emotionally stable guy in the supermarket might pass you right by without a second glance. Who knows? You've basically just spent the day telling the rest of the world that you barely have the energy to put on pants in the morning. That you're invisible. And exciting, positive things rarely happen to the invisible.

My experience tells me that human beings don't want to be ignored. And they don't want to be mistaken for hookers if they're not. And they don't want people to think they're lazy if, in reality, they are working their asses off. They don't like missing opportunities for more money or more love or more respect.

When you align your visual message with who you really are as a person, life falls into place. I promise. I've seen it happen a hundred times. (Of course, other factors come into play. If you're a jerk, a pretty wrap dress isn't going to fix the fact that no one likes you. And if you're depressed, you should see a therapist.)

I am also reminded—with each and every makeover I perform—how damn difficult a true transformation is.

So, I just want to get this out of the way now: If you are unwilling to put effort into your appearance, you might as well just skip this section. Go make some beautiful decoupage plates or a lovely cassoulet (pages 145 and 64, respectively), because there is no way to go from a hot freakin' mess to a chic, fabulous creature without some amount of exhaustion, frustration, and maybe even a good cry.

Now, I'm not saying you look like crap. Maybe you do. I don't know; I can't see you. What I'm saying is that the best way to approach improving your style is by baby steps—and by changing your mind-set. It does not require a huge investment to have a fabulous wardrobe. Does it help? Sure. But money does not guarantee good style. I promise you from the bottom of my blackened heart that if you put in the mental and physical effort, you can look better than you ever imagined.

Freakin' Fabulousness

1 CREATE *a* FASHION BUDGET

When you spend money willy-nilly, you're going to have a much more difficult time looking fabulous, because you will end up with a closet full of mismatched pieces. It's very easy to walk into a store and get caught up in sale this and sale that: "Oh my God, I can't believe this is seventy-five percent off! I must buy it!" Or even if you go into a thrift store, and you're like, "Oh, just look at all this stuff that I can get for five dollars!" Stop it! Dressing well on a budget is not about bargain shopping; it's about

smart shopping.

You have to have to have to wrap your head around the concept that if a garment does not fit you, it does not flatter you! If it cannot be tailored to fit you, then it is *worthless*. WORTH LESS. And therefore, if you spend anything on it, you have wasted your hard-earned money—whether you spent $5 or $500 or $5,000.

Now's when I get all Suze Orman on your ass. The first step of good style is to buy clothes responsibly. You must examine your total yearly income and create a realistic BUDGET. How much of your income is ESSENTIAL to put a roof over your head and food in your family's mouth? How much does your transportation to work cost you? Are you spending money on education?

Don't these questions SUCK? I know, I know. I've always hated budgeting too. But the truth is, you have to do it, just like going to the dentist or cleaning the toilet. (Truth be told, I like both of those things, but I'm a freak.)

Once you know how much you need, you'll know how much you have left to spend on NONESSENTIAL things, hopefully things that will make you happy—like movies, the cable bill, dinners out, an occasional show, belly dancing lessons, crafting supplies, etc.

Where do clothes fit into the equation? Are they essential or nonessential?

I say, a little bit of both. You *need* clothes to protect you from the elements and an indecency arrest, so some of your clothing budget should fall into the essential category. But only you can decide what is more important to you. Is a well-fitting, attractive wardrobe more essential than a fifth flat-screen television for your house? What's more important: work-appropriate clothes that send the message that you deserve a promotion or buying your kids another Wii game? Children are not going to be better human beings because you bought them the latest tech gadget, but you will be better able to provide for your family if you have a wardrobe that helps you get ahead in your career.

You need clothes to have a job, to make money, to carry out your profession. Your wardrobe is absolutely an investment in you as a person. It's in our DNA to size up each other by appearance. When we were cave people, Thorg needed to size up Erg very, very quickly: "This friend or foe?" People who couldn't size up others with enough haste were eliminated from the population . . . because they were eaten. It's pure Anthropology 101. (You're welcome.)

Now, go do some math and get back to me. I'll wait.

That was quick. I figured you'd take much longer than that, but you clearly have a better head for math than I gave you credit for—apologies for underestimating you. Okay!

How much do you have to spend on clothes per year: 200 bucks? 500 bucks? 1,000 bucks?

Once you've got your number, the simplest way to divvy up your fashion budget is to spend 70 percent on classic clothes and 30 percent on trendy pieces (I'll define "classic" in depth soon). Of course, the ratios will go up and down depending on your age and profession. (You might need more trendy items if you work in a creative field or more classic looks if you're in your forties and beyond.)

COST *Per* WEAR

New math, old math, whatever! **Fashion math** is the only math you'll ever need. I'm talking about **Cost Per Wear,** people. The value of a garment is the cost divided by how many times you wear it, and it's represented mathematically like this:

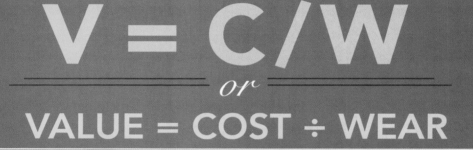

$$V = C/W$$

or

$$VALUE = COST \div WEAR$$

If you buy a well-made blazer that gives you a lovely womanly shape for $120 and wear it 50 times, that's $2.40 per wear. But if you buy a blazer for $40 because the price tag looks good, yet the blazer does not—either it is cheaply made, not really your style, or too trendy—you may wear it twice. That blazer cost you $20 per wear.

See what I'm getting at here? Let's try one more.

You invest in a well-made designer pair of jeans that flatter your figure and make you look like a million bucks. The price tag: 140 smackers. Hello, sticker shock! You wear those jeans 2 to 3 times a week for one year. That's about 140 wears, and that's easy math—$1 per wear!

Then one day you buy a pair of discount jeans at an outlet store for 50 bucks. The fit isn't quite right, but, hey, what a bargain! You wear those jeans 4 or 5 times and then they get tossed to the back of the closet: $10 per wear.

The opposite can also be true. If you buy a trendy piece for $300 because of the name on the label, but it doesn't flatter your figure and you wear it only once or twice, well, then, you've blown it. You could have had two pairs of great jeans.

I know, I'm a modern-day Einstein, with better hair.

The RULE of TWOS:

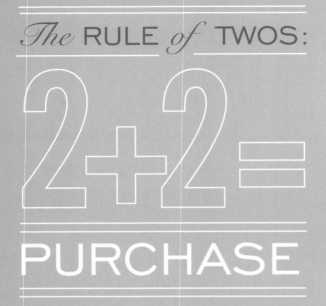

2 + 2 =

PURCHASE

This rule always makes me think of Chuck Woollery on *Love Connection*: "We'll be back in two and two!" Oh, the spectacle of TV dating before the Internet.

THE FIRST "2" is the idea of being able to wear something in two different aspects of your life. So, every garment that you buy—at least most garments that you buy—should be able to fit into two categories of your life—work, weekend, and evening. This purple jacket wouldn't be a smart purchase if it could only be paired with jeans. But here, the model (who happens to be my styling assistant, Julia) makes it work for an office outfit with an olive shirtdress as well as an evening look over a shiny top. There are lots of possibilities here.

The idea behind the LBD, or little black dress, is that it can be worn to work with a cardigan, which would be removed for an evening out. Another example: a blouse that you can wear to work with a pencil skirt, that you can also wear on the weekend with a pair of jeans. *Magnifique!*

When nothing works together, you end up with a closet full of clothes with tags on them and a wallet full of regrets. By implementing the Rule of Twos, your clothes are providing you with a great value and you are creating multiple fabulous looks from less.

THE SECOND "2": You must already have two other things in your wardrobe to pair with a piece. Often women buy stuff on sale: "It's a forty-percent-off flash sale! Grab everything!" And when things are at a discount, all logic flies out the window: "Oh, this is a beautiful printed skirt! This royal blue with splashes of green and orange is so exciting!" But then you get home and the truth sets in: You have nothing in your closet that could possibly go with the multicolored skirt. That's a problem. To make a budgetworthy purchase, you need to own two pieces it will go with to create an outfit.

2 STAGE *a* CLOSET CLEANSE

I won't lie. This process might be more painful than a colon cleanse. But I'm telling you, this exercise will

change your life.

Go into that closet. Pull every freakin' article of clothing out of it and throw it onto the bed, the dining room table, the sofa. Whatever you have to do, just get it out of the closet. Then, meticulously and honestly, go through piece by piece, and try everything on.

If it is too big, it gets thrown into the "too big" pile. If it is too small, it gets thrown into the "too small" pile. If it just fits, it gets its own happy, special pile. There's also a little pile for things that are slightly too big or that need a little alteration.

So, if it's more than a size too big, it goes in the thrift store pile (or rather, the pile for your favorite charity or consignment store). If it is too small, get it out of the house ASAP, because clothes that are too small remind you that you are no longer that size anymore. And it's mental torture for you to go into your closet and be reminded on a daily basis that you're no longer a size 4, and that you are now a size 8.

"Oh, but Clinty, I keep those tiny shorts around to inspire me to lose weight," you say as you bat your eyelashes and take a bite of a Twinkie. Lots of people do this, and you know what? It never f#$^ing works. Pardon my French. It's just making you feel worse. Ditch your "skinny clothes," my fabulous friends,

and get rid of your "fat clothes" too. Because those fat clothes give you permission to go back up to an undesired weight, and that is unacceptable.

Stop sabotaging yourself.

Once you've weeded through all your clothes, let's see what you're left with. These are the articles of clothing you actually have to work with. And my Lord! Looking at this pile of "keeper" clothes makes you realize that you're stuck in a rut—a horrible rut that you never noticed. Just where did those ten teal shirts come from and why are all of your pants black, tapered leg, and covered in cat fur? This is my cue to run screaming from your home. I suggest you join me.

3 KNOW THAT FIT *is the* ESSENCE *of* STYLE

Before heading out to shop, you must understand and commit to memory that a huge part of dressing *Freakin' Fabulous on a Budget* is that you're not going for the label, whether it's high-end, low-end, or in between. The number one factor is fit. Do your clothes fit and flatter you? Do they tell the world what you want the world to know about you? All the rest of the stuff is cockadoodie. Women with money and great style (the two are not mutually exclusive) know that fit means everything.

American Women : You are living in a fantasyland.

I have delightfully met thousands of you lovely ladies across the country, and more often than not, you presume that you will walk into a department store, look at the perfectly dressed mannequin, try on that very ensemble and look sensational, buy it with a 20-percent-off coupon (good today only!), and go home to make sexy time with your lover on a bed of rose petals.

This only happens in chick lit. Have you ever looked at the backside of a mannequin? The clothes are all completely pinned up, twisted, and pulled to look perfect. So, if the clothes on the rack don't even look good on the proportionally "perfect" mannequin, how will they ever look perfect on you? All I'm saying is: Be aware. Nothing is as perfect as it seems.

CLINTON'S
COMPREHENSIVE
Tailoring Guide

Tailoring is not a pain in the **tush.**

In fact, it can make your bum look better. Invest the time and money in some nips and tucks, and it will allow you to create pieces that fit you *Freakin' Fabulous*-ly.

We already know that clothes that fit well look like they cost mucho moola. My tailor's name is Ewa, and I would never look as fabulous as I do without her needle and thread. Find a skilled tailor and cling to him or her for dear life. A good tailor will be able to re-create pieces to mask your trickiest body parts. It's best to buy clothes that fit your most "difficult" body part and then have them altered in other areas. For example, if you carry your weight in the midsection, finding clothes that fit can be particularly difficult, just because clothes are generally designed on an hourglass dress form and that tummy is really the opposite of an hourglass. So, when it comes to tailoring, you've got to work around your middle.

Let's say that your belly causes you to be a size 14, but the rest of you is an 8. When shopping for a jacket, you'll probably have to buy a size 14, and then have the shoulders taken in or reset and the sleeves shortened.

Don't get confused! Here is a simple guide to what can and can't be done to the most essential pieces of your wardrobe.

PUT *Your* BEST BREASTS FORWARD

If you haven't already done so, go get a professional bra fitting. I wish I had a nickel for every time a woman emailed me asking where to get a professional bra fitting. I don't know, because I don't know where you live! Use Google. But I do know that you should have it done by someone who fits boobs for a living, not some high-school chick making seven bucks an hour at the mall after school. Ideally, the majority of your bust should rest halfway between your shoulder and your elbow. That's where boobs are designed to be, in clothes. If your boobies aren't where they need to be, clothes will never really fit you properly. Invest in a well-fitting bra and your wardrobe will take on new value, because suddenly clothes will sit on your body that much better. If your boobs don't land halfway between your shoulder and your elbow naturally, don't feel bad about yourself. That's the whole point of bras. If every woman had breasts that naturally floated between the shoulder and the elbow, no one would need a bra, and hetero-sexual men would walk around all day praising the Lord.

179

YOU CAN . . .

1. Reset too-large shoulders. Shoulder seams that extend past your anatomical shoulder will often result in a messy upper sleeve and make you look like a kid in a school play wearing her mother's jacket.

2. Add a small shoulder pad to balance a large bust or balance out a tummy. We're not talking about 1980s shoulder pads à la Joan Collins. But a little bit can really strengthen the shoulder and deemphasize the bust and belly.

3. Have the sleeve shortened so that it hits you at the wrist, not the hand.

4. Take it in on the side seams or from darts under the bust to create a waist that balances out a large bust.

5. Add darts in the front of a jacket for more of an hourglass shape.

6. Take a jacket in through the back seams for better fit.

pad?

easy one!

7. Narrow the sleeves. There is usually a seam that runs down the inside of the length of the arm, starting at the armpit. When taken in, it creates a great separation between the arm and the midsection, which will help your body look like more of an hourglass.

8. Add a vent in the back, either single or double. If a woman has a larger tushy, and the jacket isn't sitting right, a vent adds wiggle room.

9. Move buttons over on a too-tight jacket.

10. Add a little hook and eye between buttons. Let's say your jacket has two buttons, and it's gaping a little bit because of a large bust, belly, or that's just the way it hangs. You can have a little hook and eye put in between those two buttons to keep it closed.

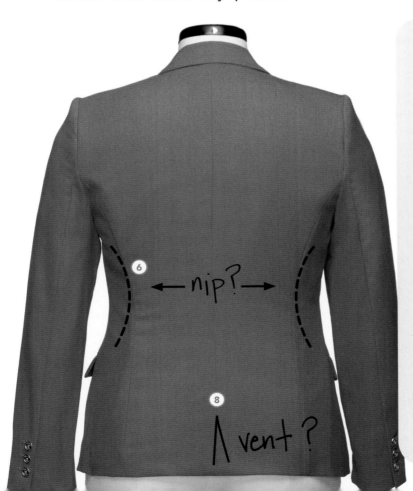

6. ←nip?→

8. ∧ vent?

DON'T BOTHER . . .

- Shortening a jacket. It will never come out the way you want it to, because it always looks a little off. If it has a curved hem, it's a lot harder to take up than just a straight sort of squared-off hem.

- Removing buttonholes. You can't just sew a button-hole together and pretend it was never there. It's like an appendix scar. You can sew up the hole, but it's still there. (Ten years after my appendectomy, I am still traumatized.)

sew 'em ② shut?

YOU CAN . . .

① Take them in at the waist. That's the most common alteration. If you have a large butt and a small waist, the gap in the back of the waistband needs to be closed. Either the band is taken in a little in the middle or two darts are created in the waistband in the back. Often, when pants don't fit at the waist, you suffer from a nasty case of dropped crotch. Taking in the waist will help them sit in the right places overall.

② Remove all pockets and have them sewn shut! If you carry any weight in the hip or behind area, the pockets can add bulk and they just look messy. Who wants to see a crumpled swatch of fabric bulging out of your ass cheeks? Pants look more expensive minus the pockets, anyway.

③ Let them out at the waist. This is a good option if you're sort of an in-between size and the pants are just too tight to be comfortable. But it only works if there is enough extra fabric. It is always easier to have slacks taken in rather than let out.

④ Remove the pleats. Snatch those dated herringbone trousers from your closet and update them in a flash, by ditching the pleats. You and your pants will instantly look more modern and streamlined. It's not the cheapest alteration in the world, but it might be cheaper than buying new trousers.

⑦

5. **Take them in through the seat.** Suffering from pancake tush? It's one of the more difficult things to dress around, because pants are constructed to make room for a butt. But you can remove some saggy fabric in the rear.

6. **Take in the sides.** Ladies lacking in the hip department often aren't able to fill out the pants. Yes, trousers come with built-in hips! Taking them in down the side seam will streamline the look of your leg.

7. **Let out the hem or make pants shorter.** Pants should be half an inch off the floor. It's best to have pants for heels and pants for flats, so the hems don't drag on the ground or look too short with different shoes. Sometimes you can find a happy medium. If you're only going to do a two-inch heel, it's not the end of the world to hem your pant to go with flats. But if you're the type of woman who likes to wear four-inch heels, you really have to have your heels trousers and your flats trousers.

8. **Remove the cuff.** Don't like the look? Get rid of it. But you can't add one. There won't be enough extra fabric and there's really no reason for it.

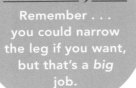

Hot Tip

Remember . . . you could narrow the leg if you want, but that's a *big* job.

OR

183

YOU CAN . . .

1 Do pretty much the same alterations on denim that you do on pants, but since the fabric is thicker, it's difficult to take them in through the seat. Unless you're dealing with a lightweight denim trouser, pass on a pair that needs to be taken in through the seat.

2 Have your tailor maintain the original hem of your jeans when you need them shortened. Otherwise you get that look of "Mom did these for me over the summer break." NOT FREAKIN' FABULOUS.

DON'T BOTHER . . .

• Hemming bootcut jeans more than an inch. If the jeans are way too long on you, they're seriously meant for a taller person, and when hemmed, the knee area won't be properly positioned. It's going to end up lower on your body than it should be, so the proportion of the denim is all screwed up like some funky, weird bell-bottom thing. You also won't be able to reattach the original hem because of the difference in diameter of the new hem.

nip in 'round back

sew shut?

add 2 darts here if there's a zipper here

YOU CAN . . .

1 Take a skirt in at the waist.

2 Shorten it to fit.

3 It's hard to say what the length of a pencil skirt should be. A lot of it depends on body type and what kind of shoe you're going to be wearing it with.

DON'T BOTHER . . .

• Taking in a pencil skirt along the side seams. Sure, it can technically be done, but why bother when a skirt in another size or from another manufacturer will give you a more streamlined look.

dart ?

The ideal silhouette ends just below the kneecap, but a petite woman wearing a flat shoe can get away with a pencil skirt hemmed just above the knee.

4 For an A-line skirt, you can have it hemmed to fall just below the kneecap or at mid-kneecap.

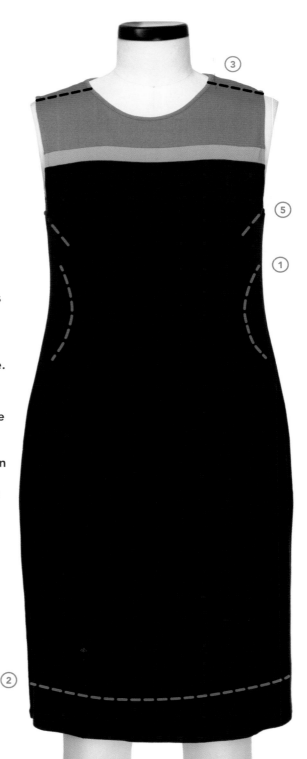

DRESS

YOU CAN . . .

Do so many things! Oy, where do I start?

1. Take it in through the waist for a more hourglass look.

2. Hem it.

3. Shorten the straps! If you have a short torso or if you're petite, shortening the straps of a dress might be one of the easiest ways to improve the way a dress falls on you.

4. Add a snap or a stitch to decrease the amount of cleavage.

5. Put in darts to close up a gaping armpit if you don't have a big bust and you're not filling out the dress (especially if there's no stretch in the material). Darts create shape. They sort of tighten it up where the fabric comes together. The tailor just removes some of that fabric and sews it back up again.

hidden
snap

④

①

②

②

YOU CAN . . .

1. Add darts to create more shape, especially if you have a small bust **1A**. Sometimes adding darts in the back is helpful if you have a very small frame **1B**.

2. Velcro tabs or small snaps between buttons also work to keep the shirt lying flat.

3. Shorten sleeves—but make sure that the tailor maintains the cuff and that the tailoring is done from the top of the cuff.

DON'T BOTHER . . .

- If you have a really big bust and a really small waist, button-front shirts really aren't your best friends. Sorry. You can have darts or snaps added to keep the shirt placket from rippling and gaping, but for the most part, you're going to feel like your boobies are about to bust out at any moment.

YOU CAN . . .

1. Shorten a hem. And why would you bother doing that? Because sometimes a shorter blouse can make you look taller and thinner. If you're wearing a blouse untucked and it completely covers the crotch, you will immediately look shorter. It just happens. When your legs look shorter, you look shorter, and when you look shorter, you look wider. If this is a concern for you, have blouses hemmed to mid-hip. A lot of women are now saying out loud to uninterested spouses, "What does that mean, mid-hip?" And I say, "Give yourself a karate chop on the hip. Where would that karate chop be?" That's mid-hip!

2. Curve a hem. Sometimes hemming a top so that it is a little shorter on the sides than it is in front and back (a shirttail hem) can provide tush coverage while maintaining a long leg line.

Both of these blazers cost less than $40, but one looks droopy and ugly, while the other looks chic and professional. Which one would you buy? Let's break it down together. I will now dissect this garment to show you how one looks chintzy, while the other passes for pricey.

LOOKS CHEAP

WRINKLE-PRONE FABRIC

BOXY

NO DETAILING

ONE BUTTON DOES NOT DEFINE WAIST

BULKY POCKETS

DROOPY SHOULDERS

TOO-WIDE SLEEVES

BLAZER:

A SHOWCASE SHOWDOWN

- LOOKS CHIC
- BETTER-QUALITY, UNWRINKLED FABRIC
- CURVED SEAMING PROVIDES HOURGLASS SHAPE
- TOUCHES OF LACE PANELING LOOK EXPENSIVE
- FOUR BUTTONS PROVIDE SHAPE
- NO BULKY POCKETS
- STRUCTURED SHOULDER GIVES BALANCE
- NARROWER SLEEVES

ANOTHER UPGRADE:
If the buttons are chintzy-looking, they can easily be replaced with classic buttons.

CLOTHES THAT HAVE SHAPE ALWAYS LOOK MORE EXPENSIVE THAN THOSE THAT JUST HANG THERE, OR DROOP, OR ARE VACUUM-SEALED TO THE BODY.

CHOOSE a STYLE ICON

Artists have muses, and why shouldn't you? When you're new at something (like dressing fabulously), it means you are an apprentice. You need somebody to look up to, to learn from, someone who does what you want to do better than you know how to do it.

Fun Fact: When I was growing up, my style icons were Mr. Rogers and Gene Rayburn of *The Match Game*. It's true. Why? I love a cardigan, like Fred, and I love mixing prints, like Gene!

A style icon, or group of style icons, can help you spend money more wisely until you have a rock-solid sense of your own style. For example, if your style icon is Gwyneth Paltrow, you can ask yourself every time you shop, "Is this something Gwynnie would wear?"

White cross-trainers? Probably not.

Drapey silk blouse? Yup!

Multichain necklace? Sure!

Handbag made from two beer cans and some fishing line? Not over her dead body.

Sure, it sounds a little silly, but I promise it can help you zero in on pieces that will propel your own style forward while encouraging you to pass by the rest. And, quite frankly, it's pretty damn fun to do when shopping.

Assignment time! Go find your icons and do some research on them. Don't just choose, say, Bonnie Tyler because you're a huge fan of "Total Eclipse of the Heart." (Who isn't, really?) Go online and search for images of your ideal fabulous person. Or maybe it's someone you actually know!

Your great-aunt Mildred, your boss, your best friend! What is it about their style that appeals to you? Is it a color palette, a knack for accessorizing, an often-worn silhouette? I love the idea of someone who decides her style is 25 percent Courteney Cox, 50 percent Jackie Kennedy Onassis, with a little bit of her fashionable Grandma Tess thrown in.

Take your time and get creative.

There is one big problem with having a style icon, about which I shall now warn you, dear reader: Performing artists wear clothes meant to get a lot of attention—because they're literally onstage and/or trying to drum up publicity for their projects. You, however, are not selling albums or blockbuster movies. I meet a lot of young women who say things like, "I want to look like Pink!"

What? She's a multiplatinum singer and you work part-time in a tanning salon. Pink's style works for her. It's made her rich and famous. What is Pink's style doing for you besides reminding you that MTV isn't exactly beating down your door?

Also, your icon needs to have a body type similar to yours. You can't really be a size 18 petite and look to the Olsen twins for inspiration. Sorry. That might be a drag to hear, but it's true. They can wear anything because they're built like petite coatracks. Same goes for the reverse. If you're flat as a board, is Sofía Vergara really the wisest iconic choice for you?

However, sometimes you can combine icons to make them work for you! Here's how I created some modern looks using fabulous style icons as springboards.

AUDREY HEPBURN'S
Timeless Elegance

+

TINA TURNER'S
Rock 'n' Roll Flair

+

Loves to Layer Jewelry

=

ERIN

KATE MIDDLETON'S
Graceful Femininity

\+

MARILYN MONROE'S
Sultry Sex Appeal

\+

Lady Who Lunches

=

SALLYANN

BEYONCÉ'S
Flashy Attitude

+

REESE WITHERSPOON'S
Country All-American

+

GREAT-GRANDMA INEZ'S
Handmade Bag

=

JULIA

TAYLOR SWIFT'S
Fresh and Flirty Vibe

+

MICHELLE OBAMA'S
Ladylike Sophistication

+

Hoedown Honey

=

TAKISHA

KATHARINE HEPBURN'S
Powerful Presence

+

ANNE HATHAWAY'S
Tailored Polish

+

Must Have Glitter

=

JULIA

5 CHOOSE CLASSIC CLOTHES

When you're shopping on a budget and want to look expensive, you need a healthy dose of classics.

Classic clothes are the cornerstones of any good wardrobe. Why? They look moneyed. So, no matter whom you have chosen as a style icon, no matter how you have defined your personal style, some portion of your wardrobe must be of the classic ilk. If money were no object, you might be able to get away without classic pieces. You could wear the most modern, avant-garde pieces every day and look pretty damn expensive. But let's face it, if money were no object, you wouldn't have bought a book with "budget" in the title.

What is classic? I point you to some of my favorite style icons: Audrey Hepburn, Jackie Kennedy Onassis, and Grace Kelly. Even Mary Tyler Moore. If you were to analyze their styles, you'd discover a few common denominators: Their clothes fit them really well—really well— ahem, tailoring! They also wore a lot of clean lines, preferring simple silhouettes to elaborate, frilly ones. Their accessory choices were always very focused—maybe a giant necklace but never a giant necklace and chandelier earrings. Oh, the horror! (Well, *maybe* for a banquet.)

STYLE GAMES *with* CLINTON

Another game that I like to play with myself—I like to play with myself, okay?—is "How much money is this worth to me?" I don't even look at price tags when I go into a store. I can't be bothered. Instead, when I see something that catches my dazzling blue eyes, I try it on. And I say to my fabulous self, "Clinton, this blazer looks really good on you. And the fabric is kind of nice, and it doesn't have to be tailored. Plus, I can wear this with five other things in my wardrobe. It works for evening and weekend. Therefore, I declare that this blazer is worth $300 to me."

Then I flip the tag over. If it's $300 or less, I will buy it.

And if it's $350, I say, "No, thanks. I'm outta here!"

Try it. live it. love it.

You Win!

To look expensive on a budget, you must know what

expensiveness

looks like, so that you can copy it! Get your butt out of the house and into expensive clothing stores.

Is that a little intimidating? Sure. But, God Bless America, you can shop wherever the hell you want. I mean, don't walk in eating a cheeseburger and start touching the cashmere sweaters. Wash your hands and appreciate the quality of the craftsmanship and discover what fancy-schmancy designers are doing to whip fashionistas into a froth.

Whatever you do, don't get too excited and buy anything you can't afford. And by all means, don't feel bad about your funds. The idea is to see how to create a very upscale look on your lower budget.

Designers knock off looks all the time! And that's your duty when shopping on a budget—to take a high-end look and completely knock it off by doing it in a budget-savvy way. Stop playing the typical game: "I like to go in and save as much money as I possibly can." Screw that. Change the game into "I'm going to create an outfit that looks like it cost $5,000, but I'm going to do it for $75."

Don't let designers and retailers have power over you. You are 100 percent in charge of your own look. If you think a blouse is worth $50 but the chichi boutique has it for $100, then screw them. Save your money and find the blouse somewhere else for $50. . . . Mind-blowing moment: It's really flipping the whole shopping experience on its ear! The designers are not in charge. The retailers are not in charge. You are in charge of your budget, and your look, 100 percent!

The CLASSIC CANON

You should probably have these wardrobe staples in your closet.

- (A) **EVENING CLUTCH**
- (B) **PENCIL SKIRT**
- (C) **HEELS**
- (D) **TRENCH COAT**
- (E) **DARK DENIM JEANS**
- (F) **BOOTS**
- (G) **LITTLE BLACK DRESS**
- (H) **DAYTIME DRESS**
- (I) **AN EVERYDAY PURSE**
- (J) **COTTON BLOUSES WITH SEAMING AND DETAILS**
- (K) **WALKING SHORTS**
- (L) **SANDALS**
- (M) **CARDIGAN**
- (N) **DENIM JACKET**
- (O) **FLATS**
- (P) **COLORFUL COCKTAIL DRESS**

CLASSIC *or* NOT?

THE OUT-OF-STYLE FORMULA

How can you tell if something is a classic? Here's a general rule of thumb: If you can imagine yourself wearing it five years ago, it will probably be in style five years from now. If you can imagine yourself having worn a version of it twenty years ago, some version of it will probably be in style twenty years from now. Try thinking this way the next time you go shopping. It's really helpful when you're standing at the register about to pay for your purple leather walking shorts.

5 EASY PIECES

There are five pieces of clothing that say, "I'm a schlump, and I've given up." I shake my head in shame every day knowing that so many Americans waste their hard-earned cash on schlocky clothes. But here I come to save the day! I have budget-friendly upgrades that will have you screaming, "I'm *Freakin' Fabulous* and I know it!"

look at this disappointing creature

She dresses for "comfort," with no concern for her appearance or dignity. She's shamefully sporting the five biggest fashion offenders: a hoodie sweatshirt, light-wash jeans, a shapeless T-shirt, a backpack, and white cross-trainers.

oy!

By upgrading these cop-out clothes, she will instantly boost not just her appearance but also her confidence. And after she's invested in my five upgrades, she will be able to form multiple ensembles, thereby getting more for her money.

The gray sweatshirt is history. If you have more than one sweatshirt and one hoodie in your closet, get rid of them! Start replacing them with casual completer pieces, like a cotton-canvas, leather, or denim jacket. Cardigans, too!

So long, light-wash jeans. Polished, dark-wash denim free of distressing, rips, or tears will always look more expensive.

Throw out every shapeless, unisex T-shirt you own. Opt for a blouse with seams, darts, and details. I think the word *blouse* scares some women; it makes them think of an elderly relative. But a blouse is just a shirt that is cut for a woman! It doesn't have to be silk, charmeuse, or any fancy fabric. It just has to have a little bit of feminine detail to it.

Backpacks—they're good for *lugging around heavy textbook*s. If you're worried about your back and shoulders, lighten the load in your bag and opt for a tote or a cross-body bag. A couple of shoulder presses now and again wouldn't hurt either.

Cross-trainers—this is probably the most pervasive mistake happening in America right now. I don't know where the hell people got the idea that it was okay to wear cross-trainers at all times. I blame Jerry Seinfeld. The shoe always, always, always sets the tone for an outfit. And cross-trainers say that you are a tourist. A tourist in your own land!

Speaking of tourists, there are few things that make me cringe more than sitting at a sidewalk café in Paris, sipping a café au lait, and spotting a gaggle of Americans, all pointing at the Eiffel Tower and all wearing white cross-trainers. Aaaargh! My skin crawls just thinking about it!

They're fine for the gym (or when you're eighty-three), but for everyday life, there are better options!

Ladies, how about a flat?

A non-athletic sneaker?

A boot?

A sandal?

Great shoes can elevate an outfit by a solid 2 points on a scale of **1** to **10**. Meaning if an outfit is an **8**, the right shoe can make it a **10**! If your outfit is a **3**, you're S.O.L.

How to Shop
THRIFT *and* CONSIGNMENT STORES

If you are the type who might walk into a secondhand store, spy a lace-and-fur jumpsuit, look at the label, and exclaim, "Oh, wow, this is Alexander McQueen! I don't have to pay full price, so obviously it's worth it!" then please never set foot again in a thrift shop. Also, I suspect you probably have one too many pet ferrets.

Shopping consignment takes a lot of diligent rummaging and repeat visits to scout new merchandise. In my opinion, thrift shopping should not involve picking through a pile marked "$1 per pound!" That's how I buy produce, not clothes. I also believe consignment stores are best for buying classic pieces that stand the test of fashion time and that can easily be mixed with more modern pieces.

When shopping in these types of places, you need to hold clothes up to the same standard as you do clothes in department stores and boutiques. They need to be in good condition: no rips, no tears, and no odors. Lord, please, no odors. A good consignment shop wouldn't even stock BO-doused garments. Examine the clothes as if you are a forensic detective: Does the zipper work? Is the lining in shreds? Don't feel shy about turning pieces inside out; the salesperson has seen it all before.

Here are a few examples of how to make vintage finds work:

Julia and I found a brocade suit for $30. When she tried it on as a two-piece suit, she reminded me of a 1970s housewife on her way to pick up her teenage daughter from after-school detention. Not exactly the look she was going for. So we decided to break it up, pairing the jacket with dark-wash denim for a sassy evening look. We hemmed the skirt to mid-knee—it was mid-calf—eeeew—and now it's the easiest skirt in the world to pair with a classic blouse for work.

Freakin' Fabulous
STYLE ETIQUETTE

Never tell anyone how much you paid for anything. It's tacky (unless, of course, you're chatting with a close relative or best friend). When somebody says to you, "Oh, I like your top," just accept the compliment graciously and say, "Thank you." Don't blurt out, "Oh, thanks! I got it on sale for $19.99!" The person who complimented you may have assumed you bought it for $150, so now you've just cheapened your look by 130 bucks. That's quite a discount! Sometimes the less people know about you, the better. It makes you mysterious and interesting. Do you know what I'm wearing right this second? No, you don't. And I'm gonna let you assume it's a custom-made cashmere Snuggie.

I found the dress SallyAnn is wearing at Goodwill for $13. It's a brand I had never heard of, but the silhouette is pretty straightforward; it's got a V neck with a little knot at the bust and a flared skirt. And I thought the brushstroke print was pretty, the kind of print you might see on a Diane von Furstenberg dress. It was in perfect condition—no rips, holes, stains—so we bought it and added a white denim jacket, a metallic bag, and some simple peep-toe pumps. The whole outfit cost less than $100, and every piece can be mixed and matched with other items in SallyAnn's closet. If we had gotten all caught up in the need for a recognizable designer name, we would have walked right past this. When thrift shopping, it's imperative that you judge the garment on its own merits, not on the designer's reputation or lack thereof. Any piece you buy should be in "like new" condition and, most important, fit you really well.

Takisha and I found the nautical-inspired blazer she's wearing at a thrift store for just $15. I liked the seaming and the trim on this jacket because they make it look more expensive. It's a brand sold in a store known for carrying trendy pieces. But be careful about buying really trendy pieces in thrift stores: They're usually in the thrift store because the trend has passed. However, while the "nautical" trend might come and go, classic tailoring and detailing never really go away. All-American looks (the type Ralph Lauren is known for) and military-inspired pieces tend to have more longevity than other trends. Takisha will get many wears out of this jacket over the years, making it a super value.

CHEAP TRICK

If you're not the savviest shopper in the world, take advantage of the free personal shopping services in department stores. There's no catch. Really. Tell them you need pants and you're on a budget, and they'll pull out a bunch of pants in your price range. That's their job! Trust me, having someone scurry around the store for you makes shopping a lot less painful. Plus, a good personal shopper will call you as soon as things go on sale!

COME CLEAN

I love doing laundry. I could do it all day (except for folding, which I find incredibly tedious). Washing your clothes wisely will help your clothes last much longer.

Here are my some of my BEST TIPS to clean up your laundry routine.

1 I am not a fan of traditional deodorant because it contains aluminum. Luckily I don't give off much BO, but I do wear it because working under hot TV lights all day can make me work up quite a man-sweat. So, before chucking my clothes in the hamper, I do a sniff test. Could I get away with wearing these jeans again? Will I clear a subway car if this sweater is not laundered immediately? **WEAR CLOTHES MORE THAN ONCE WHEN AT ALL POSSIBLE.** Save money on water and electric bills and give a knowing nod to Mother Nature for lending you her valuable resources.

2 My vision of life in the Italian countryside is highly romantic and involves fields of cypress tress, bottles of Chianti, and naughty uses for fresh-pressed olive oil. But there is always the image of big, white bloomers hanging on the line in the courtyard. They are not my skivvies, rest assured, but could belong to any one of the beautiful local ladies. Americans are hooked on their dryers. The rest of the world likes a little sunshine in their underpants. **HANG CLOTHES TO DRY** whenever possible outside or on an indoor rack. Your electric bills will go down south, and your clothes will last much longer!

3 Make sure you have enough dirty laundry to **MAKE A WASH WORTH-WHILE.** Unless that small pile of putrid socks is stinking up your bedroom, it's more cost-effective to run a reasonably large load instead of lots of tiny ones. But don't overload the washer—your clothes need room to groove; otherwise the grime will just get redeposited on your garments and you will be the smelly chick at work.

4 **VINEGAR** can lightly dress salad greens, but in your washing machine it takes on a whole new life. Add a cup to the wash cycle to soften clothes instead of using pricey liquid fabric softener. It will also freshen musty loads of towels (everyone has them, do not be ashamed). Your pantry holds a bevy of other natural laundry products too. Salt removes stains, lemons whiten whites, and baking soda neutralizes odors.

5 **DITCH EXPENSIVE DRYER SHEETS** made with questionable chemicals and opt for woolen dryer balls. Like a good masseur, they are reusable and will pummel your clothes silly till they are soft and wrinkle-free. A good collection could last up to five years. Forgo the plastic versions you might see in the grocery store and troll the Internet for ones handmade by Brooklyn-based hipsters who refuse to acknowledge that they have multimillion-dollar trust funds and don't really have to craft woolen balls for a living.

The BAG

Don't just lust after labels. Often, what makes a bag look expensive is its classic shape. Here's how to achieve the *style* without the *price tag*.

CAN'T AFFORD *this* $$$ GUCCI BAG?

So what! Look for a leather day **CLUTCH** with metallic accents.

CAN'T AFFORD *this* $$$ CARLOS FALCHI BAG?

So what! Look for a flat-bottomed, cylindrical **BUCKET** bag.

CAN'T AFFORD *this* **$$$ GUCCI BAG?**

So what! Look for a rectangular, zip-top, two-handled **BOWLER** bag.

fabulous

CAN'T AFFORD *this* **$$$ YSL BAG?**

So what! Look for a half-moon-shaped **SATCHEL** with two long handles to fit over your shoulder.

fabulous

CAN'T AFFORD *this* **$$$ HERMÈS BIRKIN BAG?**

So what! Look for a squarish **STRUCTURED** doctor's bag with distinctive hardware closures.

The BAG *(continued)*

So what! Look for a **CROSS-BODY** bag, which is smaller than a messenger bag, and meant to carry just the essentials.

So what! Look for an envelope-shaped **CONVERTIBLE** bag. It should have a strap or a chain you can tuck inside.

FF fabulous

So what! Look for a softly constructed, long-strapped **MESSENGER** bag.

FREAKIN' FABULOUS *on a* BUDGET

214

CAN'T AFFORD *this* **$$$ BOTKIER BAG?**

So what! Look for a soft and slouchy crescent-shaped **HOBO** bag.

CAN'T AFFORD *this* **$$$ LOUIS VUITTON BAG?**

So what! Look for an open-topped, long-handled leather **TOTE**.

LOSE *the* LOGOS

I hate to break it to you: That teeny-tiny logo bag you're carrying around in your armpit isn't impressing anyone. The $5,000 bag from the same company might look expensive, but the $100 logo bag . . . not so much. It's really an unfabulous message you're sending: It's like you care about labels, but you can't afford them, so you'll settle for whatever you can get your hands on. I hate to use the D-word, but I will. It looks desperate.

   This holds true for clothes too. Why would you wear a T-shirt with Armani emblazoned across the chest? Do you think for a second that anyone who can actually afford an Armani Privé gown would be caught dead in the tee? No freakin' way—unless they're getting a kickback. So if a company isn't paying you to wear its logo, then don't do it.

The FINISHING TOUCH:
ACCESSORIES

The right accessories can add hundreds of visual dollars to your look. The wrong ones can cheapen you faster than a door-buster holiday sale. Here are a few things to think about when adding those finishing touches.

The JEWELRY

Stop piling on the tchotchkes. Lots of dinky jewelry doesn't add up to looking like you have money—it looks like $5 plus $5 plus $5 equals $2. It says: Look at all the jewelry I can afford to pile on me! I'm so awesome!

The best way to wear jewelry is not to prove you are rich by doing a big earring and a big necklace and a big bracelet and a big cocktail ring. Choose one piece to make sure that other people's eyes go to the one impressive object.

It's fine to buy matching earrings and necklaces if you love a specific design or stone. But there's no rule that says you have to wear them together. Back in the day, women had to match their jewelry. Don't ask me why. So, the biggest reason not to wear matchy-matchy jewelry is that it makes you look like an old bag. The only exception: diamonds. They match everything.

Let's NECK!

HOW TO WEAR NECKLACES

The key to successful neck accessorizing is to avoid a competition between the garment's neckline and the necklace itself. They should peacefully coexist. No confusion over where one starts and one ends. No fighting for attention. No getting tangled up in each other.

LET ME SHOW YOU SOME EXAMPLES:

Long chains work well with a high neckline.

Pendants tend to work well with V-necks. They should hang so as to evenly fill the triangle of skin created by the dress or blouse. Round chains and multistrand necklaces can also work here, provided they don't sloppily overlap the V.

Round chains work well with square necklines, as do bold-statement necklaces.

A scoop neck takes a round chain or several layered chains nicely.

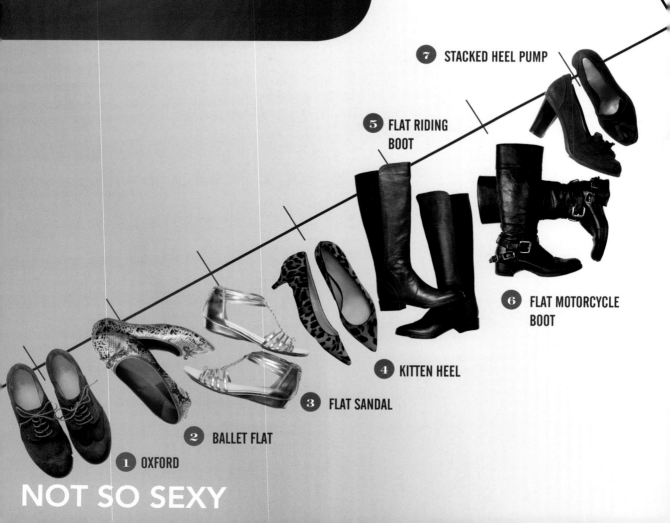

The SHOES

Truth be told: Sometimes it's really difficult to tell an expensive shoe from an inexpensive shoe—even for a fabulous style expert like myself. BUT (and I like big "buts") the shoe always, always, always sets the tone for an outfit. So before you slip something on those cute little tootsies of yours, be sure to consider the vibe you want to exude. Here's a handy sex-appeal chart for your feet.

7 STACKED HEEL PUMP

5 FLAT RIDING BOOT

6 FLAT MOTORCYCLE BOOT

4 KITTEN HEEL

3 FLAT SANDAL

2 BALLET FLAT

1 OXFORD

NOT SO SEXY

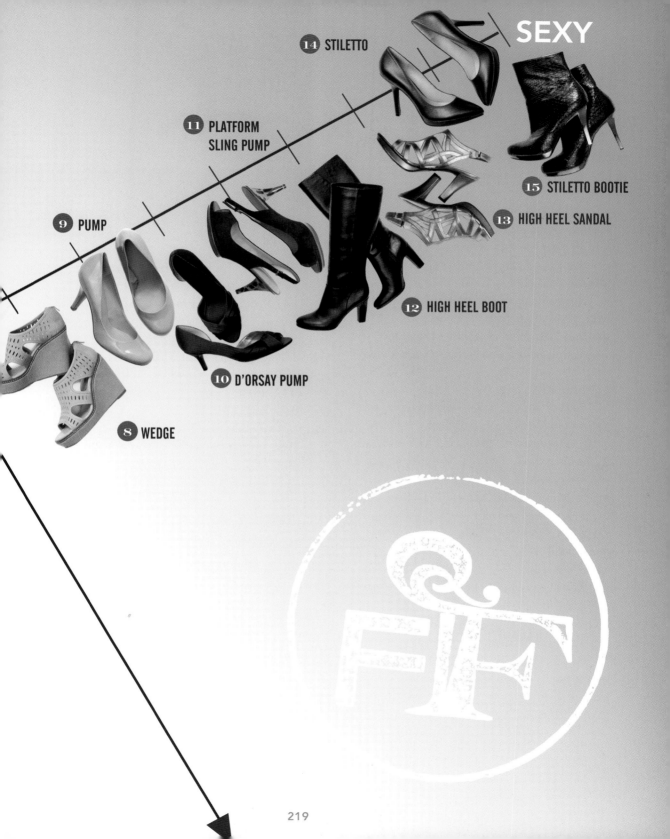

14 STILETTO

SEXY

11 PLATFORM
SLING PUMP

15 STILETTO BOOTIE

9 PUMP

13 HIGH HEEL SANDAL

12 HIGH HEEL BOOT

10 D'ORSAY PUMP

8 WEDGE

MAKE OVER *Your* MAN

Having done *What Not to Wear* for a decade, I am 100 percent convinced that you cannot change someone who does not want to be changed. So, if your husband has no desire whatsoever to look good, he's probably a lost cause. And if his appearance repulses you to your core, divorce him.

But sometimes an opening occurs! If your guy ever makes comments like, "Oh, that guy has great style," or "I wonder where that handsome Clinton Kelly fellow gets his clothes," there's your window of opportunity to help him!

First of all, don't overwhelm a man with too much information. Start with one little thing, and when he gets used to it, move on to the next. For example, if he only wears sneakers, see if you can convince him to try a nice pair of suede loafers. Then treat him like a dog. You know how you train a dog? You praise it like crazy when it does something right. And you give it a treat. When he wears the suede loafers out to dinner with you, tell him several times over the course of the night how good he looks! Then, when you get home, give him a treat.

The next time you're getting ready to go out for a bite, he won't even *realize* why he's slipping into his new soft shoes, kind of like a dog that has learned to automatically fetch your newspaper.

look at this hapless fellow!

He's so lost, and frankly, his clothes make him appear invisible. Like his female counterpart we met a few pages ago, he is trapped in the "I give up" nonfashion zone. Note his shlubby hooded sweatshirt, light-wash tapered jeans, shapeless shirt, and ubiquitous athletic cross-trainers. This guy represents the dashed hopes every woman has experienced on a blind date.

"You set me up with this dud?!"

I will now wave my *Freakin' Fabulous* wand and transform this man into the sharp dresser that he— like all of you— deserves to be!

Sad.

TRY THESE:

Here are the cornerstones of a stylish man's wardrobe: a nonathletic sneaker, boot, or loafer; polished, dark-wash jeans; a somewhat fitted button-down shirt with seams; and a casual jacket or structured blazer (the unfussy kind, not the type your accountant is wearing, which I suspect is navy with gold nautical-themed buttons).

The transformation is priceless but doesn't have to run up your credit card debt. With these key pieces you can help rebuild your man's wardrobe.

DRESS *Your* AGE:
FOUR MAJOR MISTAKES TO AVOID

There's a certain point in every woman's life when she will ask herself,

"Am I too old to be wearing this?"

And if you have to ask the question, the answer is . . . **MAYBE.**

The fact that you're even asking yourself the question is a good sign. It shows you're not a complete nutbag. At every stage of your life, you must analyze and question what works for you and what doesn't. And that could mean when you're thirty, not just sixty. The next time you encounter a beautiful item in the store and it gives you pause, run through these four criteria so you don't waste your money on clothing that is totally inappropriate.

1. Does it show too much cleavage for daytime wear?

2. Does it show navel?

If you've ever been to South Beach, you've probably seen a grandma with a dangling belly button piercing. It's not cute. Just leave your abdomen covered.

A woman over "a certain age" can sport some cleavage, but it's best to bring out the boobies in the evening. You don't want to be showing too much soft tissue during the day because it looks like you're trying too hard, like you're hoping to attract a man with your breasts, or worse, you didn't realize that your knockers are hanging out and everyone is just too polite to say something. And let's face it. Most women at, say, forty-five don't have the same kind of perky décolletage that they had when they were twenty-five. Let the younger girls show off their ta-tas while they're still buoyant. A good rule of thumb for daytime—and especially for the office, no matter what age you are—is "chest, not breast."

3. Does it show too much leg?

You might think you've got the best legs in the world for a woman your age. Bravo for your confidence! I'm sure your gams are great, but you might be setting yourself up for a competition you can't win. Let's say you buy a minidress and you wear it to your cousin's wedding. You're on the dance floor shaking your groove thing. Next thing you know, your eighteen-year-old niece and the bride's twenty-three-year-old sister start dancing right next to you. Oh, and they're wearing minidresses too! Duck, duck, goose. Someone's legs don't look as good as she thought they did. You just set yourself up for a hot-leg contest and lost.

Look, I'm not trying to make you feel bad about yourself. Women are beautiful at all ages, but you never want people to be whispering, "Oh, look at Aunt Agnes trying to be young and cool." Keep hemlines just above the knee and save your luscious legs for the bedroom.

4. Is this a good outfit for a hooker?

You really want to make sure that you're not participating in any trend that a hooker might look at and say, "Now, that's gonna get me some more customers!" Let tramp trends pass you by. A woman after a certain age should not be leading with sex. She should really be leading with her beauty and her brains! It kind of sucks to hear that, and I feel sucky just writing it, but I want to be very clear about this. An older woman *can* be sexy. However, after a certain age, confidence is sexier than skin. Please know that you have more to offer the world at this point in your life than just a pair of tits.

> #### The PARTY'S OVER
>
> My most important age-related rule has nothing to do with fashion, but I want you to know, when you're the oldest person at the bar, it's time to go home. Yes, even I abide by this one, even when I don't want to. Last time I went out for drinks in Boston, I was in my hotel room by 8:30. Too many damn college kids. I felt like the lame uncle who thinks he's cool.

Beauty
on a BUDGET

You can't look like a million bucks with caterpillar eyebrows or poppy seeds in your teeth. Here are **nine ways** you can appear to look more expensive via simple grooming.

1. EYEBROWS ARE THE ULTIMATE. A well-groomed, perfectly arched set that frames your face is the most important thing a woman can do for herself. A shaggy pair can bring your whole look tumbling down. I've run into friends whom I have not seen in ages and gasped with pleasure at their fabulous appearances. And it's always the eyebrows. They just make the rest of you look sensational. Go to a professional shaper. Have her set the stage and you can maintain from there, splurging on occasional touch-ups. There is not a gal on Park Avenue who hasn't memorized the cell number of her eyebrow guru.

2. SMILE! Oy. I think you have a little escargot stuck in your front tooth. *Très* uncouth. People with expensive tastes and the bank accounts to back them up would never spend a minute with food in their teeth or have red-wine-stained chompers. Healthy, white teeth and fresh breath are signs of common hygiene we should all adhere to. Brush and floss twice daily, use a whitening paste, crunch on fresh veggies, and sip water (I prefer sparkling) after each meal to flush away any leftover bits.

3. I'm a huge believer in the RESTORATIVE POWER OF SLEEP, especially after age thirty. It's hard at any age to look fabulous with droopy eyelids and dark circles under your eyes. Getting adequate rest keeps you looking young and healthy. Rather than staying up late to watch TV, turn in early and let your cells repair themselves so tomorrow you look rested and gorgeous. You say you can't fall asleep? No caffeine after 3 p.m. and stop using your bed for anything other than sleep and sex.

4. Nothing says "cheap whore" like long red acrylic claws. Nothing says "street urchin" like ragged, dirty nails (acceptable only if you are a farmer). I have a happy medium for you: NEAT, MANICURED FINGERNAILS, not too long and slightly squared. No time for polish? Ask for a buff manicure in which the technician rubs your nails with a special cloth until they are shiny, natural, and presentable.

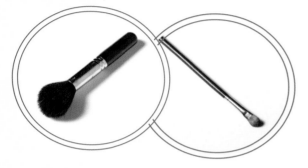

5. I'm fine with drugstore makeup. I'm not fine with the sad little brushes that come with shadows and blushes. INVEST IN A DECENT SET OF MAKEUP BRUSHES and you will be able to apply pigments more effectively. When you try to pile colors on, it just looks overworked and skanky. Little foam "brushes" can do that to you.

6. There are lots of creepy rumors out there about what fancy people use to keep their skin dewy and radiant: nightingale poop, caviar, earthworm kaka, and snail slime. Rich folk have the time and money to get regular facials (and regular sleep), but they can keep their questionable ingredients all for themselves. A GENTLE FACIAL CLEANSER, sheer foundation, and some well-placed brightener will all go toward helping you achieve a luminous air.

7. I don't think women were allowed to graduate from finishing schools in the old days unless they could balance a book on their heads for an ungodly amount of time. I won't ask you to perform such a feat, but EXCELLENT POSTURE is the sign of a moneyed upbringing. You'll look better in clothes (and thinner!) when you stand tall with your shoulders back.

8. Between summers in Ibiza and winters on the slopes of Aspen, ladies who lunch get a lot of sun exposure. But it makes no difference where you catch your rays, as long as you don't let them age you. Please USE A FACIAL MOISTURIZER WITH SUNSCREEN, and don't forget to treat your hands and chest. Those two spots are vulnerable to sun and can quickly give you a weathered façade.

9. Peeling lips are gross. No one wants to kiss them. You might be dehydrated, overexposed to the elements, or living in a superdry New York City studio apartment. Whatever the cause, fix it. And WEAR A RESTORATIVE LIP BALM night and day till you have a smooth pucker. I have never seen a high-society grand dame with a flaky mouth.

BATS *in the* CAVE & OTHER FIRST-WORLD PROBLEMS

Your friend has what appears to be a booger from outer space taking up half a nostril. Your boss has a piece of spinach in her teeth so big it looks like she's missing a bicuspid. A random guy walking down the street has forgotten to zip up after his last tinkle. **WHAT DO YOU DO?**

Oh, I hate situations like this! How I wish we lived in a world without pee, poop, ear wax, boogers, blood, eye gunk, phlegm, BO, or farts. Maybe in my next life I'll be reincarnated as a freesia. I'll sprout from the ground, bloom into gorgeousness, and then die.

ALAS, I'M A HUMAN—HEAR ME TOOT.

HERE'S HOW I RECOMMEND YOU HANDLE OTHER PEOPLE'S PROBLEMS.

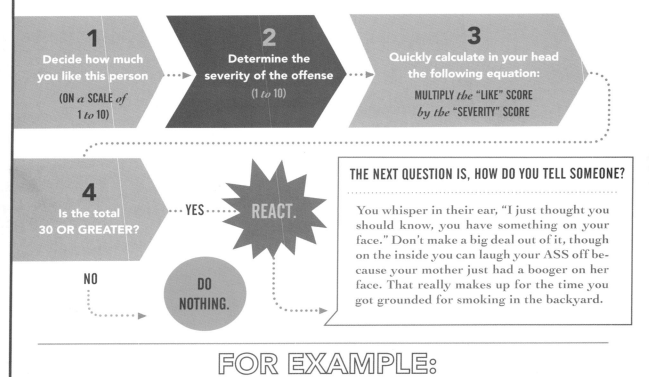

1 Decide how much you like this person (ON *a* SCALE *of* 1 *to* 10)

2 Determine the severity of the offense (1 *to* 10)

3 Quickly calculate in your head the following equation: MULTIPLY *the* "LIKE" SCORE *by the* "SEVERITY" SCORE

4 Is the total 30 OR GREATER?

YES ····· REACT.

NO

DO NOTHING.

THE NEXT QUESTION IS, HOW DO YOU TELL SOMEONE?

You whisper in their ear, "I just thought you should know, you have something on your face." Don't make a big deal out of it, though on the inside you can laugh your ASS off because your mother just had a booger on her face. That really makes up for the time you got grounded for smoking in the backyard.

FOR EXAMPLE:

- If my mom (whom I love, so that's a 10) had a booger on her cheek (very severe = 10), that would be 100 points (10 × 10). So I would definitely tell her.

- If a kind-looking stranger (5) has a piece of toilet paper stuck on her shoe (6), 5 × 6 = 30, so you would tell her.

- If a boss that you can't stand (1) has a case of extreme halitosis (9), 9 × 1 = 9, so you would not tell him.

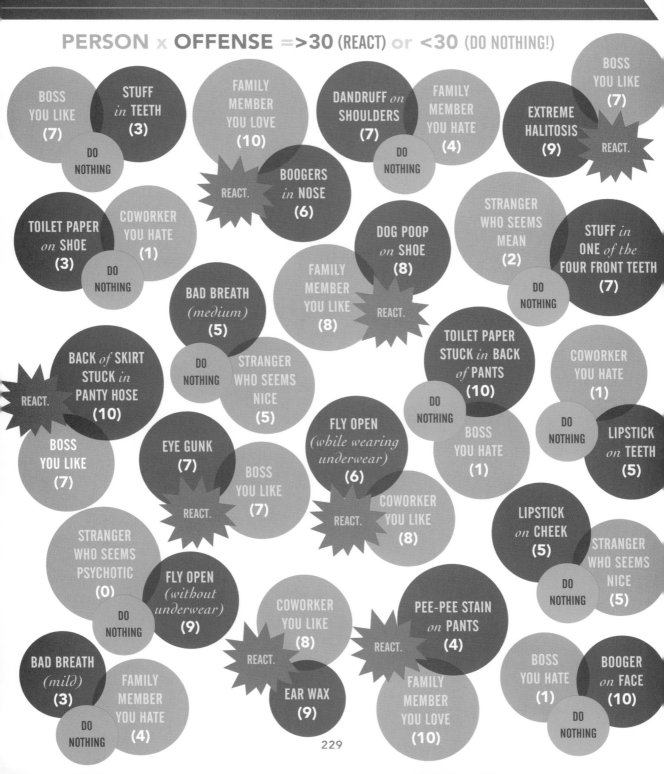

HERE ARE SOME MORE EXAMPLES TO WORK OUT YOUR OWN FORMULAS:

PERSON x OFFENSE =>30 (REACT) or **<30 (DO NOTHING!)**

229

speaking and writing with style

THE I'S DON'T HAVE IT

There's no such word as I's.

Do you want to come to Fred and I's house?

WRONG.

My mom and I's recipe for snickerdoodles is great.

WRONG.

Sally and I's baby is gonna be real smart.

WRONG.

The word you're looking for is:

my

Do you want to come to Fred's and my house?

My mom's and my recipe for snickerdoodles is great.

Sally's and my baby is going to be smart.

Granted, this all sounds pretty fussy.
You're better off just rewording the whole sentence.

Do you want to come to our house?

Our recipe for snickerdoodles is great.

Our baby is going to be smart.

YOUR Fabulous.
Um . . . No.

PLEASE, I beg of you, learn to use the word **YOUR** correctly in your written correspondence—whether it's a letter to Grandma or a tweet to Lady Gaga.

Every time you write *your* when it should be *you're,* God rips the wings off an angel. (Aww, that image made even me a little sad, but I'm keeping it in to make a point!)

THE WORD "YOUR" IS A POSSESSIVE. IT IS USED TO DESCRIBE SOMETHING THAT BELONGS TO YOU.

Your epiglottis.

Your Chihuahua.

Your crush on Ryan Gosling.

"You're" is a contraction— that is, two words smushed together to make one word, in this case the words *"you"* and *"are."*

SO "YOU'RE" SHOULD BE USED ANYTIME YOU ARE ACTUALLY SAYING "YOU ARE."

You're a knucklehead.

You're standing on my underwear.

You're one sexy beast, Clinton Kelly.

Pop Quiz! FILL IN THE BLANK WITH THE APPROPRIATE YOUR OR YOU'RE.

_____ best friend called me yesterday. She said _____ no longer invited to her birthday party because of _____ behavior at last year's party when you flashed _____ butt to her grandma. She said _____ a drunk, but I tend to disagree. I think _____ a good-time kind o' gal, and _____ ass looked fabulous.

ANSWERS: Your, you're, your, your, you're, you're, your

To MUCH

Another grammar mistake that gets my old knickers in a twist is the misuse of *too* and *to*. I see it every damn day on Facebook. Your seventh-grade English teacher spent a solid week on this subject, but evidently you were too busy daydreaming about getting to first base with anyone other than a member of the Dungeons and Dragons Club.

LET'S GO OVER THIS AGAIN:

TO

is mostly a preposition. It does a lot of things, like expressing motion or helping to specify a relationship.

FOR EXAMPLE:

I'm going to the proctologist. He is related to me. Weird!

TOO

is an adverb that describes an amount that is more than enough.

FOR EXAMPLE:

I smoked too much Maui Wowie. So, I ate too many brownies.

Too can mean "also."

You're sleeping with him too? Better get checked for the clap.

Pop Quiz! STATE WHETHER TOO OR TO IS USED CORRECTLY IN THE FOLLOWING SENTENCES:

1. Dear Clinton, you are to fabulous for words.
2. I would love to spend some time with you on a deserted island.
3. You could braid my hair and we could talk too each other for hours and hours.
4. I'm getting to excited just thinking about it.
5. My cell mate keeps telling me to shut up.
6. When I get out I'm coming to get you. Love, Bernice.

Answers: incorrect, correct, incorrect, incorrect, correct, correct (and illegal)

"ITS"
DRIVING ME
BONKERS

One more little grammar pet peeve. Next time you are posting on Facebook, consider the difference between *its* and *it's*.

IT'S is a contraction of two words: **IT** and **IS**.
So, it can be used whenever you say, **"IT IS."** FOR EXAMPLE:

> It's my birthday.

> It's not a lie this time.

> It's sad that I didn't receive enough attention as a child.

ITS without an apostrophe is a possessive, so use **ITS** to express the fact that something belongs to **"IT."** FOR EXAMPLE:

> My pet monkey pooped its pants.

> My pet snake shed its skin.

> The Department of Health left its phone off the hook.

Pop Quiz!
MULTIPLE CHOICE. CHOOSE THE SENTENCE IN WHICH IT'S OR ITS IS USED CORRECTLY.

A. Your ego is so big it has it's own zip code.
B. That old Cosby sweater doesn't hold its shape.
C. Are you sure its supposed to hurt that much?
D. Its a shame about your flare-up.

Answer: B

Well, dear reader, I'm not sure there's much left to say. The rest is up to you.

GET OUT THERE AND REACH FOR

FABULOUSNESS.

Will it be exhausting? **YES.**

Will it be frustrating? **PROBABLY.**

Will you say to yourself when trying on the twelfth pair of pants that do not fit,

"Self, why am I not at home right now eating pizza rolls on the couch while watching Honey Boo Boo?"

Sure, that might just cross your mind.

If it does, tell yourself,

"Self, there's someone out there who thinks I'm worth it. And his name is Clinton Kelly."

ACKNOWLEDGMENTS

I would like to extend my thanks to the
following freakin' fabulous folks for their help
in making this book possible.

THE WOMEN OF GALLERY BOOKS:

TRICIA BOCZKOWSKI, JENNIFER BERGSTROM,
and JENNIFER ROBINSON.

You're all so damn smart and cool and fun. Let's make babies together!
Not real babies, little papier-mâché babies with bonnets made
from wonton wrappers.

THE WOMEN OF CLINTON KELLY, INC.:

JILL BILLANTE, JACKIE HAMADA, *and* JULIA HILL.
Thanks for working so hard at all things CK.
You're a bunch of superstars, even if I do mess up your names all the time.

MY LONGTIME LITERARY AGENT, LAUREN GALIT.
You've known me the longest of anyone on this list! Wow! Tell them
what a dork I was back then and I will tell everyone how old you are.

PHOTOGRAPHER STEVE GIRALT.
Dude, you are so chill and insanely talented. And you're not even
slightly nuts. That is really rare for a photographer.

GRAPHIC DESIGNER JANE ARCHER.
You're the best at what you do! And you always look like your hair
smells pretty. One day I might venture a sniff.

ALONNA FRIEDMAN.
For a mom of two, you have an incredibly firm hiney.

GABRIELLE VOIGT-CINQUEMANI.
You've bought and furnished a home, because I need so much help
from the neck up. Stick with me for another eight years and you
should be able to buy a palace.

credits

Book Producer: Jill Billante; **Photographer:** Steve Giralt

FOOD

Food Stylists: Martha Tinkler, Jackie Rothong

Prop Stylist: Francine Matalon-Degni

Shot of Clinton: p. 57 Apron from lestoilesdusoleilnyc.com. ***The Perfect Cheese Plate:*** p.13 Platform No. "Nineteen" cheese platform from montesdoggett.com. ***The Perfect Antipasto Platter:*** p. 15 "250c plus" platter from asa-selection.com, tray from zak .com. ***Dumplings:*** p. 17 "Apero" white plate from asa-selection .com. ***Freakin' Fabulous Fondue:*** p. 19 Fondue bowl and skewers from shopmastrad.com. ***Marinated Olives:*** p. 27 "Color It" plate from asa-selection.com. ***Spiced Chickpeas:*** p. 31 "Club" martini glass from sagaform.com. ***Lemon-Roasted Asparagus Wrapped in Prosciutto:*** p. 41 Plate No. "Fifty-Four" from montesdoggett .com. ***Boeuf Bourguignon:*** p. 59 "Vongole" bowl from asa-selection.com; "Spectra" glass from sagaform.com. ***Braciole:*** p. 61 "250c plus" platter from asa-selection.com. ***Cassoulet:*** p. 65 "250c plus" square casserole from asa-selection.com. ***Chicken Cordon Bleu en Croute:*** p. 67 "Color it" plate from asa-selection.com. ***Salmon en Papillote:*** p. 75 "Spectra" glass from sagaform.com. ***Apple Crostata:*** p. 83 plate and bowl from asa-selection.com. ***Boozy Shakes:*** p. 85 Tray from zak.com. ***Cherry Clafouti:*** p. 89 "Color It" plate from asa-selection .com; towel from lestoilesdusoleilnyc.com; ***Grilled Fruit:*** p. 95 "Spectra" dessert bowl from sagaform.com; ***Strawberry Napoleons:*** p. 99 "Cucina" platter from asa-selection.com. ***Frozen Sangría:*** p. 107 "Juicy" tray, "Juicy" and "Aloha" glasses from sagaform.com. ***Old-Fashioned:*** p. 109 "Frida" glasses from crateandbarrel.com. ***Sidecar:*** p. 111 "Club" glasses from saga form.com.

DÉCOR (CRAFTS!)

Craft Stylist: Kirsten Earl

Prop Stylist: Francine Matalon-Degni

Color-Blocked Table Runner and Napkins Made from Shirts: p. 121 Cacharel dinnerware by Kiyasa, available at Michael C. Fina and Saks.com; "Spectra" wineglasses from saga form.com; Mikasa's "Italian Countryside" flatware from mikasa.com. ***The Most Amazing Wall of Art:*** p. 142 Pillows from judyrosstextiles.com. ***Bamboo Screen:*** p. 146 Chair and pillow by Prudence Designs, prudencedesignsnyc.com. ***Eglomise? What the Heck Is That?:*** p. 148 "Spectra" wineglasses from sagaform.com; chairs and pillows by Prudence Designs, prudencedesignsnyc.com. ***Large-Format Art—for Cheap!:*** p. 156 Chair from Prudence Designs, prudence designsnyc.com. ***Paint Yer Balls! and Let's Get Conical:*** pp. 164, 166 Apothecary jars from abigails.net, 800-678-8485; tablecloth from Secrets de Provence at The Accessory Collection, 407-260-8010.

STYLE

Fashion & Style Director: Julia A. Hill

Styling Assistants: Erin Dempsey, Kirstin Aimée, Laurel Allyn

Special thanks to: Macy's, Zappos.com, Lia Sophia, Jennifer Miller Jewelry, LOFT, and the following models: SallyAnn Thibedeau, Takisha Walters, Rebecca Billante, Erin Dempsey, Julia Hill, Anthony Subietas

Shots of Clinton: p. 177 Heel by Nine West, provided by zappos.com; jacket by INC, provided by Macy's; dress by Dorothy Perkin's; jewelry by Lia Sophia. p. 205 Hat (stylist's own), iron provided by Steve Giralt. ***The Rule of Twos: 2 + 2 = Purchase*** pp. 174–75: Model: Julia; (Work) Blazer by Gap; dress by Jones New York, provided by Macy's; heels by Nine West, provided by zappos.com. (Evening) Blazer by Gap, top by Old Navy, shorts and tights by H&M, ankle boots by Old Navy, clutch by Co-Lab, jewelry provided by Lia Sophia. ***Clinton's Comprehensive Tailoring Guide*** pp. 178–89: Blazer by Vince Camuto, provided by Macy's; pants by Gap; jeans by Style&co.; pencil skirt (stylist's own); A-line skirt by Carmen Marc Valvo; sleeveless dress by J Jill; red dress by White House Black Market; button-front shirt by Jones New York, provided by Macy's; blouse by Express. ***The Cheap Blazer: A Showcase Showdown*** p. 191 (Looks Chic): Blazer by Style&co., provided by Macy's. ***Style Icons:*** p. 193 Model: Erin; Jacket W118 by Walter Baker, provided by Macy's; top by Zac Posen for Target; pants (stylist's own); shoes by Very Volatile, provided by zappos.com; necklace and rings provided by Lia Sophia; bracelets (model's own); Audrey Hepburn: Photofest; Tina Turner: Photofest; Necklaces image: © (pressmaster)/Crestock. p. 194 Model: SallyAnn; Cardigan by MANGO; red dress by White House Black Market; hat (stylist's own); jewelry provided by Lia Sophia; shoes by Nine West, provided by zappos.com; Kate Middleton: ©ImageCollect.com/StarMaxWorldwide; Marilyn Monroe: Photofest; Ladies at cafe image: © (v_g)/ Crestock. p. 195 Model: Julia; Jacket by Old Navy; dress W118 by Walter Baker, provided by Macy's; ankle boots by Michael Antonio, provided by zappos.com; purse (stylist's own); jewelry provided by Jennifer Miller; Beyoncé: ©Image Collect.co/Landmark-Media; Reese Witherspoon: WENN .com; Great-Grandma's image: Ann Johnson's family archive. p. 196 Model: Takisha; Cardigan Kelly by Clinton Kelly (for QVC); dress by W118 Walter Baker, provided by Macy's; ankle boots by Nine West, provided by zappos.com; jewelry provided by Jennifer Miller; Taylor Swift: © (Paul Smith/Featureflash)/Crestock; Michelle Obama: ©Image Collect.com/StarMaxWorldwide; Hoedown Honey image: © (gregory21)/Crestock. p. 197 Model: Julia; Blazer by Tommy Hilfiger, provided by Macy's; top by INC, provided by Macy's; trousers by Jones New York, provided by Macy's; heels by Nine West, provided by zappos.com; clutch (stylist's own); earrings provided by Jennifer Miller; bracelets provided by Lia Sophia; Katharine Hepburn: Photofest; Anne Hathaway: ©ImageCollect.com/Admedia; Glitter girl image: © (Kudryaska)/Crestock. *The Classic Canon* pp. 200–201: Top by Ellen Tracy, provided by Macy's; pencil skirt provided by LOFT; clutch by Nine West, provided by zappos.com; heels by Nine West, provided by zappos.com; necklace by Lia Sophia; bracelet by Jennifer Miller. Trench coat by MICHAEL Michael Kors; top by Vince Camuto, provided by Macy's; dark denim jeans by Topshop; purse by Nine West, provided by zappos.com; boots (stylist's own); necklace by Lia Sophia. LBD by Alfani, provided by Macy's; heels (stylist's own); bracelet provided by Lia Sophia. Day dress by White House Black Market; purse by Tignanello; shoes by Nine West, provided by zappos.com; jewelry (stylist's own). Cotton blouse by INC, provided by Macy's; walking shorts by Tommy Hilfiger, provided by Macy's; purse by Gap; sandals by Boutique 9, provided by zappos.com; necklace and pink/gold bracelet (stylist's own); bracelet provided by Lia Sophia. Cardigan by H&M; top by INC, provided by Macy's; pants (stylist's own); heels by Steve Madden; necklace by Lia Sophia; bracelet by Jennifer Miller. Denim jacket and dress by Old Navy; belt by H&M; purse by Rachel Roy, provided by Macy's; flats by Nine West, provided by zappos.com; jewelry provided by Lia Sophia. Cocktail dress by Vince Camuto, provided by Macy's; heels by Naturalizer, provided by zappos.com; jewelry (stylist's own). *Five Easy Pieces* p. 203: Model: Rebecca; (Top image) Jacket by Express; top (model's own); jeans by Banana Republic; boots by Nine West, provided by zappos.com; necklace by Lia Sophia; bag by Nine West, provided by zappos.com; bracelets by Jennifer Miller; ring (stylist's own). (Bottom image) Jacket (stylist's own); top by Andrew Charles, provided by Macy's; tank by INC, provided by Macy's; pants by Old Navy; purse by Big Buddha, provided by Macy's; heels by Naturalizer, provided by zappos.com; necklace and ring by Lia Sophia; bracelet by Jennifer Miller. *Shoe Alternatives* p. 204 : Flats by Big Buddha, provided by zappos.com; boots by Nine West, provided by zappos.com; sandals by Enzo Angiolini, provided by zappos.com; sneakers by Puma, provided by zappos.com. *How to Shop Thrift and Consignment Stores* P. 207: Model: Julia; (Left image) Jacket (vintage) from Housing Works; top by Jones New York, provided by Macy's; pants by J Brand (model's own); boots by Christian Siriano for Payless; necklace by Jennifer Miller; bracelets by Lia Sophia; rings (model's own). (Right image) Top by Zara; belt (stylist's own); skirt (vintage) from Housing Works; heels by Nine West, provided by zappos.com; bracelets by Lia Sophia; ring (model's own).

p. 208 Model: SallyAnn; Jacket by Old Navy; dress from Goodwill; purse by Style&co., provided by Macy's; heels (model's own); jewelry provided by Jennifer Miller. p. 209 Model: Takisha; Jacket from Buffalo Exchange; top provided by LOFT; jeans by Charter Club, provided by Macy's; boots by Nine West, provided by zappos.com; jewelry provided by Lia Sophia. *The Bag* pp. 212–14: CLUTCH: Gucci, provided by Laurie Rubin; Express; Nine West, provided by zappos.com; Co-Lab. BUCKET: Carlos Falchi, provided by Julia Hill; Big Buddha; H&M. BOWLER (clockwise): Gucci, provided by Erin Burke; H&M (white); Express; Carlos Santana, provided by Macy's. SATCHEL: YSL, provided by Erin Burke; Big Buddha, provided by Macy's. STRUCTURED: Hermès, provided by Jackie Hamada; Urban Expressions. MESSENGER: Balenciaga, provided by Allison Laskin; Gap. CROSS-BODY: Cole Haan, provided by Julia Hill; Perlina NY. CONVERTIBLE: Chanel, provided by Jackie Hamada; Olivia + Joy, provided by Macy's. HOBO (clockwise): Botkier, provided by Jill Billante; Big Buddha; Nine West, provided by zappos.com; Express. TOTE: Louis Vuitton, provided by Jill Billante; Big Buddha; Tignanello. *Let's Neck! How to Wear Necklaces* p. 217 (clockwise): Model: Rebecca; Necklace by Jennifer Miller, top by Topshop; Model: Takisha; Necklace by Lia Sophia, top by Banana Republic; Model: Rebecca; Necklace by Lia Sophia; top by INC, provided by Macy's; Model: Takisha; Necklace by Lia Sophia; top by Style&co., provided by Macy's. *The Shoes* pp. 218–19: Oxford by Very Volatile, provided by zappos.com; ballet flat by C. Label, provided by zappos.com; flat sandal by Enzo Angiolini; kitten heel by Nine West, provided by zappos.com; flat riding boot provided by LOFT; flat motorcycle boot by Mui Mui (stylist's own); stacked heel pump provided by LOFT; wedge by Banana Republic (stylist's own); pump by Nine West, provided by zappos.com; D'orsay pump by Nina New York, provided by zappos.com; platform sling; pump by Nine West, provided by zappos.com; high heel boot provided by LOFT; high heel sandal by Naturalizer, provided by zappos.com; stiletto by Nine West, provided by zappos.com; stiletto bootie by Christian Siriano for Payless (stylist's own). *Make Over Your Man* pp. 222–23: Model: Anthony; Suit and shirt by Zara; tie by J.Crew; shoes by BOSS Hugo Boss, provided by zappos.com. Blazer and button-down by Banana Republic; jeans by J. Crew; belt and shoes by Zara. Jacket and shirt by Zara; jeans by J. Crew; boots by Timberland. *Shoe Alternatives* p. 222 (clockwise): Sneakers by Zara; suede loafer by Zara; loafer by BOSS Hugo Boss, provided by zappos.com; boots by Clarks.

COLOR-BLOCKED TABLE RUNNER, p. 125
Fabric—fabric stores

NAPKINS, p. 127
Old dress shirts or shirting fabric—
  most fabric stores
½-inch or ⅝-inch iron-on hem tape—
  Walmart or fabric stores

NAPKIN RINGS, p. 129
Metallic ribbon—Michael's or most arts and
  crafts stores
Fabric stiffener—amazon.com or Michael's
Fabric glue (Fabri-Tac brand)—
  amazon.com or Michael's

REHABILITATED VOTIVES, p. 131
Straight-sided votives and cylinders—
  IKEA or jamaligarden.com
Krylon Metallic spraypaint—krylon.com

MERCURY GLASS LAMP, p. 133
Lamp base—IKEA JONSBO OROD
Krylon "Looking Glass" mirror spray paint—
  hardware stores or krylon.com

TEACUP CANDLES, p. 135
Japanese and Chinese teacups and sake
  cups—Pearl River Mart, pearlriver.com
Premium paraffin wax—Country Lane
  Candle Supplies, clcs.com or
  soapexpressions.com
Pre-wicked candle tabs for votives in large
  or medium—soapexpressions.com

LAMPSHADE, p. 137
Lampshade—IKEA JONSBO
Burlap and jute twine—jamaligarden.com

DECORATIVE TERRARIUM, P. 139
Mason jars—Walmart
Soil, sand, rocks, and plants—garden
  center stores

BAMBOO MAT ART, p.141
Bamboo mat—Pearl River Mart,
  pearlriver.com

PAINTED CEILING MEDALLIONS, p. 143
Ceiling medallions—The Home Depot or
  other home improvement stores
Krylon indoor/outdoor gloss spray paint—
  krylon.com

SILHOUETTES, p. 144
Oval frames—Michael's
Any acrylic or latex paint will work—most
  arts and crafts stores or home improvement
  stores

DECOUPAGE PLATES, p. 145
Clear glass plate—IKEA OPPEN
White plate (in same diameter)—
  Crate & Barrel
Prepressed flowers and flower pressing
  supplies—naturespressed.com
Mod Podge— arts and crafts stores
OOK deluxe plate hanger—amazon.com

BAMBOO SCREEN, p. 147
Room divider (Chinese screen)—Target

EGLOMISE TABLETOP, p. 149
Coffee table—IKEA LACK
Custom-cut glass—specialized hardware
  stores and framing shops will do this
Paint (enamel/glass paint is best for
  durability)—most arts and crafts stores or
  hardware stores

EGLOMISE SERVING TRAY, p. 150
Picture frames—IKEA

DIP-DYE RUG, p. 153
Small wool braided rug—Target
Liquid fabric dye by Rit in Fuchsia—
  amazon.com, Walmart, or Michael's

DIP-DYE VASES, p. 155
Latex paint—The Home Depot

LARGE-FORMAT ART, p. 157
All molding and remodeling materials—The Home Depot
Upholstery fabric—Mood Fabrics, moodfabrics.com

CORN HUSK VOTIVES, p. 158
Plain standard-sized votive candleholders—jamaligarden.com
Dried corn husks—Mexican food markets, or El Guapo brand corn husks available at amazon.com
String or twine—most hardware stores, garden centers, or jamaligarden.com

GOURDS, p. 161
Krylon spray paint or acrylic paint and paintbrush in colors and/or metallic—hardware stores or krylon.com
Krylon spray high-gloss coating—hardware stores or krylon.com
Dried gourds—amishgourds.com
Metallic leaf paint for stems—arts and crafts store like Michael's

GLITZY CONES AND SNAZZY NUTS, p. 163
Mixed nuts—nuts.com
Metallic spray paint in a variety of tones—krylon.com or dmcolor.com
Fine glitter—arts and crafts stores like Michael's

BALL ORNAMENTS, p. 165
Clear glass ornaments—save-on-crafts.com; also available almost all year at arts and crafts stores like Michael's
Glaze medium and acrylic/craft paints—arts and crafts stores like Michael's

TREE FORMS, p. 167
Silk dupioni fabric—fabric.com
Tree-shaped conical Styrofoam forms—save-on-crafts.com or Michael's
Black felt—arts and crafts stores (available by the piece)